FINDING YOURSELF IN
Scripture

A 90 Day Inspirational Journey

Dr. Jamal H. Bryant

D1456821

Words2Empower Publishers

Finding Yourself in Scripture, A 90 Day Inspirational Journey
1st Edition 2009 © Jamal Bryant
All Copyrights Reserved

ISBN: 10#: 0-9790213-9-1
13#: 978-0-9790213-9-8

For more information write to:
Empowerment Temple
1505 Eutaw Place
Baltimore MD 21217
www.empowermenttemple.org

Words2Empower Publishers
www.wpublishers.com
For Worldwide Distribution
Printed in Canada

Library of Congress Cataloging-in-Publication Data:
An application to register this book for Cataloging has been submitted to the Library of Congress.

1 2 3 4 5 6 7 8 9 10 / 11 10 09

Dedication:

The Bible says, *"Train up a child in the way that they should go and when they become old they will not depart from it."* (Proverbs 22:6) However if they have not been trained, they will depart. I hope through 90 days, you will receive basic training in discipline, commitment and devotion.

This book is dedicated to my daughters, whom I pray will go further and better than their father.

It is also dedicated to those who hunger and thirst after righteousness, but have been in a drought and a famine spiritually.

It is dedicated to those who want to not just start well but also finish strong!

Preface:

The greatest journey you will ever take starts with one step. Regardless of where you may want to go, you still must take your first step if you wish to arrive at your chosen destination.

A wonderful spiritual journey awaits you as you take your first step on Day 1 to read through the Bible with Dr. Jamal Bryant in 90 days. Each day Dr. Bryant offers special insights which compare situations we face in our daily lives to events which take place in that day's reading.

Psalm 119:11 says, "I have stored up Your Word in my heart, that I might not sin against You. This 90 day spiritual journey will help you to do just that.

I Can't Stop

Genesis 1 – Genesis 16

Today is the first day of a ninety day journey to read the word of God in its entirety, Genesis to Revelation. There is a great sense of zeal, enthusiasm and ambivalence.

As a visionary I am inspired because over 8000 people caught the vision and registered to walk with me through the process. As a pastor, I have concern because I know a lot of people start projects but very few finish. However I have faith in you that it will be different this time! You can not stop until you complete the journey and know YOU CAN DO IT!

Without being heretical, I realized after completing today's reading what God's problem is . . . HE CANT STOP! Philippians 1:6 says, *"He that has begun a work in you will carry it on to completion until the day of Jesus Christ".* This is the Master's work ethic. He will keep working until every thought, idea and dream is done and while He's working, He's creating, dreaming and planning some more.

In Genesis, God shows He can't stop. He creates light and darkness but He can't stop, so He creates water and the sky and still He can not stop. Next He creates dry ground, vegetation, plants, trees, and fruit, and still can not stop. This is followed by the creation of birds, creatures of the sea, livestock and wild animals. He is still not through. When He creates man, it would appear this is enough, but He still cannot stop; he must also add woman.

After the fall of man in Genesis 3:21, the Lord makes garments to cover them because it is now a habit — He cannot stop making and creating things. In verse 24, God makes fire and puts it in a sword; so the cavemen cannot even take credit for that! In Genesis 6:3 the Lord says that man will only live 120 years, but in Genesis

9:29 Noah lives 950 years. Here God makes the first exception to His word. Then because He still cannot stop, in Genesis 12:2 He makes a covenant with Abram because He has to always make something. He says to Abram, *"I will make your name great, I will make you a great nation."*

I did not mean to write this much but I cannot stop! I ask that no matter what happens over the next 89 days, do not stop until you finish the Bible. While you are reading, God will give you ideas, dreams, thoughts and revelations because He cannot stop. Do not stop until you complete the Bible!

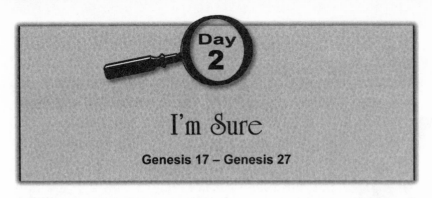

I'm Sure

Genesis 17 – Genesis 27

There was a commercial that used to air when I was growing up advertising deodorant. The backdrop was about how stress, tension and anxiety can cause one to sweat. The perspiration would leave a stain or a mark so others might be able to see the anxiety that you were under. The product advertised was SURE deodorant. The jingle to the commercial always closed with the refrain, *"Raise your hand if you're sure"*. This jingle was telling the consumer there will be no trace or sign to on lookers of the stress, worry and anxiety you are under. It promoted confidence, assurance, and security.

As I read today's reading, it occurred to me how much we have to be SURE, meaning - certain, positive and absolute. In Genesis 16, Hagar was being treated horribly by Sarai because she was bearing Abram's child. As a result, Hagar could not handle living there and ran away. The Angel of the Lord found her on the road to SHUR which says to us; being sure is a journey. Many of you are on the road to being sure about your purpose, your call, your destiny and your relationships.

In Genesis 17, Abraham is made to feel assured he will have a child even in his old age in spite of what things might look like. In Genesis 18:10, God is so sure of His power that He gives a deadline that by this time next year, the very thing Abraham did not think he would have will manifest. Are you sure God can do a miracle for you within a year's time? In Genesis 19, the Angels of the Lord were about to destroy a wicked city. Lot attempted to warn his sons-in-law of the forthcoming destruction, but they felt he was joking and as a result, they were destroyed. If only they had believed the word, they would have been saved. If you can believe the word of the Lord, you will survive so much stuff.

In Genesis 22, God tested Abraham by seeing if he would sacrifice his son as an act of love. Because Abraham trusted the Lord, his faith was honored and his son spared. Can God be sure about you in the arena of your giving all you have?

In Genesis 24, a mate was sought for Isaac by the servant. He prayed for the right person to come so that the covenant might not be corrupted. Are you SURE you are involved with the right person for your destiny?

In Genesis 27, Jacob received Isaac's blessing because he pretended to be someone else. Be SURE of who you are because what God has for you is for you!

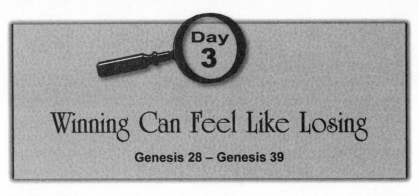

Winning Can Feel Like Losing

Genesis 28 – Genesis 39

Today, I was up early doing my reading for the day when my cell phone began to ring incessantly. Usually during study, I forego the phone or any other distraction, but something told me to answer. When I did, I was met with the news that one of my strong soldiers, Anthony Jones, had just died. Anthony has been a member of the church for almost its entire existence. He was just 21. Any person who has ever been to the church has seen him. He sits over by the choir and usually has a tube connected to his person. In spite of that, he was one of the most vocal praisers in the church. He refused to be intimidated by security or anyone else for that matter. Throughout his life, he has dealt with physical challenges that confronted his body, but never his spirit.

Recently, he just completed his high school diploma, which was awarded to him in his hospital room. As a single parent, his mother, Tonya, a faithful and committed choir member, did the job of three to five people raising him in a spirit of excellence and dignity. He asked for Ray Lewis to come visit, which he did. I had scheduled to go the day I received the call, but obviously I did not make it on time.

When the phone rang, I had just finished reading Genesis 32 where Jacob wrestled with a divine power stronger than himself. He refused to let go, just like Anthony! What bothered me and blessed me at the same time is that Jacob got a new name for being an overcomer, but he also had to walk with a limp from that point on. It only seemed right to me that since he overcame, with the new name would come good health, but not so. God has the unusual capacity to take something from you even after you overcome.

I lost a member, but I won a new appreciation for life and a greater commitment to the faith.

It's A Mix Up Not A Mess Up!

Genesis 40 – Genesis 50

I am just arriving on the wonderful island of Aruba for a two day crusade. While on the flight, a lady passed by my seat several times. She finally mustered the nerve to speak and said, "I know you! I've seen you on TV." I said, "Thank you." She said, "I love what you're doing to advance the Kingdom." I told her I appreciated it. Then she said, "My youth group loves to listen to you." I was humbled and honored. Then she said, "We buy all your music!"... MY MUSIC!?? I exclaimed, "What music? I don't have any CD's." She then responded, "I'm sorry. I thought you were Kirk Franklin!" She was mixed up.

In our reading today, Jacob was getting ready to die and asked Joseph to bring his sons so they might be blessed. Joseph presented his two sons Manasseh and Ephraim. In Old Testament tradition, the older son received the greater blessing but Jacob put his hand on the younger one — thereby breaking tradition and customs. Joseph insisted his father made a mistake, but Jacob claimed to know better.

God, in His divine grace, will break traditions and customs in your life. To other people it will seem like a mistake, but in reality God is just mixing some things up. You have now completed the first book of the Bible. Do not quit until you get to the last. There is a blessing waiting on you.

Someone asked a question, why do you sing? ... The answer is - I'm going to get a deep tissue massage on the beach (I'm not Kirk Franklin....don't get mixed up)

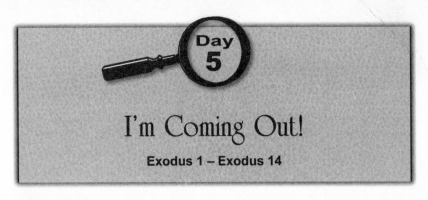

Day 5

I'm Coming Out!

Exodus 1 – Exodus 14

Today we begin reading the book of Exodus. The title by itself ought to give you reason to pause and celebrate. The root of the word Exodus comes from the word exit which means way out. Every person reading this is dealing something or another; whether it is a bad relationship, bad debt, dead end job, contentious home life, health concern or undocumented stress. It is important you connect your faith to this book; the faith to believe that when you finish reading Exodus you will be out of every crisis.

The children of God found themselves under attack in their home and job once they began to flourish and prosper. Sounds familiar? The Lord called someone (Moses), who at first glance seemed inadequate and deeply flawed. Looks familiar? (Look in the mirror) God often calls someone the enemy will underestimate and overlook. He assigned a Levite named Aaron to accompany him and speak for him. Levites are worshippers. During this Bible journey, connect with a worshipper who can speak to God for you and fight in the spirit realm with you. God hardened the heart of the enemy so that He might have an opportunity to perform miracles in front of Pharaoh. Your enemies are getting ready to have a front row seat to see God perform.

Moses lifted his hand and the situation was split in half. That is what I believe for you. If you will just lift your hands right now as you read, God has the power and ability to split your crisis in half.

* By the way - order my sermon: *He Will Walk You Through It.* The text I use is Exodus, Chapters 6 - 15, which parallels our reading for today. It will richly bless you.

Day 6

I Won't Complain

Exodus 15 – Exodus 28

One of my favorite gospel songs is entitled, *I Won't Complain*. It has become a staple in the black church tradition without being made a hymn. No choir can sing it but even as a solo, it easily transforms into a congregational selection. If you were to search Youtube under the title of the song, you will come up with three pages of people giving their own renditions of the song; some of them melodic and others catastrophic, yet all of them are sincere.

The song was released in the late eighties or early nineties from the late Houston pastor, Dr. Paul Jones. Dr. Jones was murdered in his home by burglars at the age of 30. I wish the children of Israel could have received an advance copy of the song because soon after being freed from bondage, (in today's reading) all we do is find them complaining. In Exodus 15:24, they grumbled to Moses about bitter water. The Lord heard their cry, made it sweet and produced refreshing springs (15:27). After they received water, they complained about bread (16:2). The Lord sent manna and they further complained when it turned sour the next day (even though they were instructed not to keep leftovers). Then they complain about water again (17:2). In addition, they began having complaints about each other, forcing Moses to settle disputes (18:13).

God became so disgusted that they could not get close to the glory (19:12). Our anguish will always put distance between us and His glory! Spend today complaint free! I know the reading is long but do not complain. At least you have access to the word, eyes that can see, and a mind to comprehend. I know gas prices are high but don't complain; it is a reminder you have somewhere to go. I know you do not like your job, but do not complain when unemployment is at an all time high. I know the weather is unpredictable with the ozone layer thinning, but don't complain; you could be homeless.

I'VE HAD SOME GOOD DAYS AND I'VE HAD SOME BAD DAYS! BUT AS I LOOK AROUND AND THINK THINGS OVER, MY GOOD DAYS OUTWEIGH MY BAD DAYS AND I WON'T COMPLAIN!!

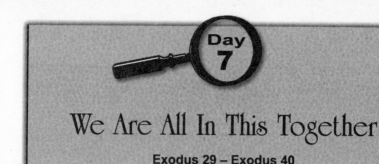

Day 7

We Are All In This Together

Exodus 29 – Exodus 40

Today we have finished the Book of Exodus and are moving onward in our journey. I pray that we all have exited out of some things along the way. But I want to take some time to encourage and remind everyone that WE ARE ALL IN THIS TOGETHER...

In today's reading, God gave Moses many instructions concerning how the Tabernacle was to be built. This is the place where God promised His Glory would dwell. There were also instructions for the Sabbath and the dedication of the Priest. In all of His instructions, God was very specific with the way things were to be done, which promised and insured the children of Israel a safe passage to the Promised Land. Even though He gave Moses the vision, plan and instructions, everyone had to come together collectively for it to come to pass.

The whole community of Israel came together to give everything needed to construct the tabernacle. Everyone with a willing heart gave so there was nothing missing (Exodus 35). They actually gave so much that Moses had to command them to stop giving because everything needed for the assignment had been acquired. All of the skillful craftsmen came together to build according to the Lord's instructions and plans. Even though the children of Israel where in the wilderness, there was nothing lacking for them to complete the God given assignment because "They Where All In It together".

This may only be day 7 of our 90-day journey and things may seem a little bit rough, but I want to remind you today, as with the children of Israel, "We are All In It together." You are not alone.

Whatever you may be faced with at this point in the journey, just remember those words. Do not get frustrated like the children of Israel in Exodus 32 when it appeared Moses was taking too long to return from mountain. Due to impatience, they decided to burn their jewelry and make a graven calf like their gods in Egypt, which was a sign of the comfort and confidence in their prior life style before the wilderness journey.

The children of Israel did have a great task and command before them to build the tabernacle of the Lord. But the one thing they had to remember was that it was going to take everyone to bring it to pass. It would take everyone's obedience to give out of a willing heart to build and furnish the tabernacle. It would also take all of the excellent craftsmen to come together to build the tabernacle and make all of the priestly garments. However, in spite of it all, they completed their task at the end of Exodus. They built a glorious Tabernacle where the presence of the Lord would reside, lead and guide them for the rest of their journey.

Like the children of Israel, God has set a great task before us even though our eyes may be getting tired and our minds a little restless. Just keep reminding yourself - We Are All In This Together and it is going to take all of us to continue on this journey.

Tomorrow starts Week Two and you should be proud of yourself. I am proud of you, but God is proud of you even more. Stay strong and focused!!!!

Do The Right Thing

Lev 1 – Lev 13

As a fellow Morehouse college brother, I am not biased when I say Spike Lee is one of the most daring, insightful, intriguing and provocative movie directors of our time. Noted for his 35+ films since 1983 dealing with controversial social and political issues like Malcolm X, his genius cannot be denied. However, one of his earlier pieces which is often overlooked, *Do The Right Thing*, holds both a message and a mandate for our community. Admittedly, doing the right thing is easier said than done. Even the Apostle Paul said: *When I would do good, evil steps in my way*.

Doing right in a world gone wrong is a true Herculean undertaking. When we closed out the book of Exodus, the glory had just settled at the foot of Mount Sinai and filled the Temple (Exodus 40:34-38). In our reading today, God is instructing Moses how to prepare the people for sacrifice and consecration. Explicit details are given on how to bring the offerings unto the Lord and what is acceptable. In the middle of that, He commanded the consecration of Aaron and his sons so they might be ready to handle the things of God. In Leviticus 8:23 God says take the blood of the sacrifice, put it on the right ear, the thumb of the right hand, and the big toe of the right foot.

The instructions were a symbolism that we might always hear the RIGHT things, hold on to the RIGHT things and stand for the RIGHT things. I pray that through these 90 days all of us will aspire to do what is right.

I know it's hard but WE can do it... (Pray for me, I'm LEFT handed)

Overview Of Leviticus

Lev 14 – Lev 25

Last night, I had the distinct privilege to read my daughter-in-the Lord, Regina Nsubuga's, notes for the small group Bible study at the church. I was so overwhelmed and overjoyed with her insight and revelation without the benefit of having gone to seminary. I am compelled to share it with you.

It would be easy to mistake or confine Leviticus to just being considered a book of the Law. This book has a bigger picture that can be easily overlooked. It tells us about God - who He is and who He wants us to be. Leviticus tells us how to cope with God's presence; how to manage it; and how to treat his presence properly. This book is about God's presence and how God will work in the midst of His people and how they are to conduct themselves.

The Law

- How are these laws relevant for the time we live in? How do we apply them in our everyday lives?

- One thing to consider is that part of Himself, who He is, and the kinds of things that are important to Him.

- The idea of holiness — God's holiness in not constricted to a single characteristic alongside others (God is love, God is kind, God is merciful, God is holy)

- Holiness is the sum total of God's characteristics and attributes. Everything He is makes Him holy.

- His holiness is what separates Him from us in that it illustrates who He is - different from us.

- When He commands us to be holy, He is mandating us to be separate from others. This can be achieved by being God like (imitating God's attributes). Reflecting Him will automatically separate us from people who live in opposition to His word. (Godlike lifestyle)

- He is holy when He is being Himself and we are holy when we are being like Him.

- The Law was designed to help the Israelites achieve that (holiness) and also handle His presence.

Holy means whole; we are to be people where nothing is missing. There should be nothing in our character or conduct which is not like Him. He makes us holy; we cannot achieve this on our own. God did not come to inspire us to be like Him, He came to make us like Him.

In Exodus, His presence came down and dwelt in the tabernacle so that He could be in the midst of His people and so that they could relate to Him. This was an initiative started by God. This initiative started back with the covenant. God took the first step to establish a relationship to begin working toward setting up His presence again. He is also in the process of revealing Himself so that we can know him and be in relationship with Him.

Revelation and Presence

The tower of Babel was man's attempt of relating to God based on their distorted ideas of who He may be. God will resolve that issue by unveiling who He is and by dwelling with His people on His terms. This process began with the covenant as God began revealing Himself and proceeds with the tabernacle as He took up residency among His people and began to reveal/show what He is really like because lots of people had distorted idea as we do.

W hat a great day to be alive! God's grace is so awesome to see what the Lord has done. Forty years after Dr. King's dream, the dream has just about been realized. As I write, Barack Obama has clinched the Democratic nomination to be the President of the entire United States of America. Even before the general election, we should pause to celebrate the primaries. On all of the news networks this morning, the analysts are trying to find a loophole as to why it is not possible to win it all. They feel the Catholics will not support him because of Father Michael Pfleger's remarks. The Bible belt will not support him because of Jeremiah Wright. The soccer moms will not support him because of Hillary Clinton. The war veterans will not support him because of John McCain. But stop the presses. In spite of it all, he is the presumptive nominee!

As I was reading the first chapter of Numbers this morning, I saw how the Lord spoke to Moses and told him to make an account of all the tribes; including their offspring, males and real estate. Beginning at verse 20 of Chapter 1, we see the tribe of Reuben, vs. 22 the tribe of Simeon, vs. 24 the tribe of Gad, vs. 26 the tribe of Judah, vs. 28 the tribe of Issachar, vs. 30 the tribe of Zebulun, vs. 32 the tribe of Joseph, vs. 34 the tribe of Manasseh, vs. 36 the tribe of Benjamin, vs. 38 the tribe of Dan, vs. 40 the tribe of Asher, and verse 42 the tribe of Naphtali. But wait and STOP THE PRESSES! In verse 47 it says the tribe of Levi is not counted!

Not being counted does not mean they did not count. The Lord did not want them counted because they were to stay in the temple and handle the tools of worship, set up the tent and guard the testimony.

When you begin to list in this economy all the things that you do not have, all that is missing and all that is wrong with your family, just remember you still have a place to worship, a place to pray and a place to hear from God. Now that has to count for something.

Slapping The Taste Out Of Your Mouth
Num 8 – Num 20

I know we live in a time where disciplining your child can now get you reported to the Department of Social Services, but unfortunately or fortunately, for most of us who were raised old school, our grandmothers refused to be co-opted by the system. If you rolled your eyes, sucked your teeth, stomped away too hard or even thought something without speaking it, you instantly became a candidate for baptism by fire. The most treasonous offense however was swearing or talking back to which inevitably you were threatened with having the taste slapped out of your mouth.

The children of Israel have become spoiled brats. In Numbers, they had a spirit of jealousy (12:1-16), they are kidnapped by fear and cowardice (14:2-38), they were upset about water (15:24-26), mad about food (16:2-8), they became bitter (16:41-50), and bothered about water again (Exodus 17:3-7); but in Numbers chapter 11 they go too far and roll their eyes, stomp around the tent and think they can dictate to God their menu and demand a buffet of quail. God had enough of it. In Numbers 11:34, God killed all those that had the craving or desire.

I am praying for you today that the Lord removes the taste from your mouth around any negative habit, lifestyle or cycle of behavior that is displeasing to God. Whatever it is that you crave, if it is more than your desire for God, I pray that it is removed and replaced with an affinity for His Word.

I know it is a battle with those cigarettes, the flesh, Internet porn, alcohol, gambling, the telephone, overeating or even the habit of being idle. However, during our walk through the Bible, I believe God is going to help your taste change!

This Is The Generation We Have Been Waiting On!

Num 21 – Num 31

I do not have much time this morning. I am in the principal's office at the Empowerment Academy preparing to give the commencement address for the 5th grade graduation. This morning's reading has stirred something in me. In Numbers 26, the plague has just been lifted for the corruption and evil that invaded the camp. The Lord gives the directive to count the new generation from every tribe that is able to go to war.

The second census of Israel was: Reuben 43,730; Simeon 22,200; Gad 40,500; Judah 76,500; Issachar 64,300; Zebulun 60,500; Manasseh 52,700; Ephraim 32,500; Benjamin 45,600; Dan 64,400; Asher 53,400; Naphtali 45,400 – for a total of 601,730 people.

We are the generation our ancestors have prayed for — poised to go from the outhouse to the Whitehouse. I must run and speak to the leaders of the next generation who are going to shape and rock the world. However, I want you to know heaven and earth have been waiting for you to seize this moment. Take it, possess it, shape it, change it....JUST DO NOT WASTE IT! We will accomplish what our parents could only dream about.

The number counted was the number going into the promise land. Make your life count by living up to your promise, purpose, and potential.

Make A U-turn

Num 32 – Deut 34

I have a dear friend who pastors in Mount Vernon, New York. A couple of years ago, he had to speak at a banquet in Atlanta, Georgia on a Saturday night. It was his intention to fly out early the next morning in order to get back for his service at 11 am. He ran through the airport and jumped on the plane with a sigh of relief; however, as the plane was taking off, the pilot announced the flight was en route to Kansas City. He began to panic because he wanted to go to New York. The stewardess extended heartfelt regrets and apologies, then told him it was the airline's policy that once the aircraft backs away from the gate, they are not permitted to make U-turns. Aren't you glad God does not operate like that?

In Deuteronomy 1:40 it say, *"As for you, turn and journey into the wilderness in the direction of the Red Sea."* Remember - they passed the Red Sea back in the book of Exodus. What should have been a journey of a couple days lapsed into forty (40) years. God escorted them into the wilderness because of their fear and lack of faith. However, now they are being put on the right road and, in essence, God is telling them to make a U-turn because they missed it or passed it. As you are reading this, there are some things in your life that you passed or missed; but because God is a God of another chance, He will give you another chance.

The key to the word U-turn is that God does not turn you; He just points you in the right direction. It is up to you to turn. *If my people who are called by name would humble themselves and pray and TURN from there wicked ways* . . . (2 Chronicles 7:14).

Barack Obama has shown us it is our turn and it is our time!

Day 14

Don't Forget About Me

Deut 8 – Deut 22

I think when everyone was younger they would all sit around as children and talk about their dreams and visions. Some of us wanted to be lawyers, others athletes, some a singer, police officer and others just famous. But one thing for certain is that we all had big dreams and plans, but we all would remind each other that once you finally made it 'Don't Forget about Me'.

The children of Israel have finally made it out of the wilderness and now stand at the brink of the Jordan; all of them ready and able to go and posses the Promise Land. One would think after forty long years in the wilderness, God would have sent the heavenly host to celebrate, blow whistles and sound the trumpets because they finally made it; but not so. The one thing He reminds them of is: 'Don't Forget about Me'. Don't forget about My laws and commandments. Don't forget that it was My grace that brought you to the Promise Land and not your goodness. Don't forget about Me when you build your houses. God tells them once they cross the Jordan and go into the Promise Land with a people they have never known, a land of good and plenty just don't forget about Him.

It is so easy for us to serve God and follow His ways when we are in the wilderness season of our lives. When everything is going wrong, we are committed and faithful. But the true test to our commitment to God is not when everything is going wrong (the wilderness) but it is when everything is going right (the Promise Land). Many of us have been faced with crisis and situations this year. It may be your health, finances, job, family or just plain problems; but through all of these problems, we have grown closer to God. Many of us now stand at the brink of the Jordan like the children of Israel about to cross over from the wilderness in to our promised land. It has been a long journey, actually much longer then we expected, bargained and prepared for, but we are about to cross over. As with Israel, God's one command for us is *Don't Forget About Me.*

I Wanna Be Your Boo

Deut 23 – Deut 34

As of today, one of the most watched videos on YouTube is the funny exchange between CNN's host Anderson Cooper and political analyst Donna Brazile. The host asked Brazile for any campaign information presidential hopeful Barack Obama might have shared with her that he has not shared with the American public. "Now Anderson, you're not my boo," Brazile answered jokingly. Cooper fired back, "I wanna be your boo".

As we read the book of Deuteronomy, it is interesting to note it feels like we have been invited to attend a vow renewal ceremony. Here we have God (the groom), Moses (the officiator) and Israel (the bride). Israel wants the benefits of being in God's presence, and relationship without meeting the requirements. The indispensable conditions of our covenant relationship with God are obedience and loyalty. Our love, affection, and devotion to Him must be the true foundation of all our actions. This entitles us to an undeniable access into His presence, which is contrasted with the curses that come as a result of our disobedience. Today, God does not want to be just the most important in your life along side others (relationships, TV, internet, food), He wants to be the only God in your life.

Literally, Deuteronomy means "second law," which signifies a repeated speaking, not of ordinary words, but of the Divine Law. The entire Bible is a Deuteronomy. As you read with me through the 90 days, you will experience a re-speaking. The word in the Bible has already been spoken, but it is re-spoken to us day by day.

In the stuff of love, none of us keep any official procedure or rituals. If we really love someone, we drop all the forms. If not, our love is not genuine. Therefore, since God has given His all, we must drop all our rituals and formalities because Jesus desperately cries, "I wanna be your boo."

It's Time To Lead

Josh 1 – Josh 14

I was raised and reared in Bethel AME Church in Baltimore, Maryland. Under the capable leadership of Dr. Frank M. Reid III, their theme and motto is, *ITS TIME TO LEAD.* Bethel AME is the oldest black church in the city of Baltimore and therefore is the head of the AME church in our area. The marching order and mandate as issued by the pastor speaks to many different levels. Bethel leads in electing more city officials any other church. It leads in merging enterprise and evangelism by partnering with Pier 6 Pavilion. It leads in innovation; pretty soon they will be the only church in the vicinity to have two locations. It also leads in its commitment to men, an ecumenism by having strong relations with both the Jewish community and the Islam community. Their theme is not limited to its parishioners, but should be a wake up call to all of us.

In our reading today, Moses is telling Joshua the same thing Rev. Reid has been preaching for 20 years: ITS TIME TO LEAD. In Deuteronomy, the Lord had already prepped and primed Moses that he would not make it to the Promise Land due to a lack of faith and a lapse in judgment. God said in no uncertain terms that a young successor was waiting in the wings. Young Joshua was a capable fighter and faith follower, but now God was changing his position from the background to the frontline. Many of you who are reading this, get ready; your position is about to change!

It is time for you to lead in every area of your life! Lead in saving rather than spending money. Lead in eating right and exercising. Lead in discipline and focus in your career. Lead in your devotion and commitment to God by praying without ceasing and studying to show your self approved. Lead by being conscience about your environment and how you consume and waste. Lead by not just giving your attendance, but also your participation in the local church.

The book of Joshua is really a handbook on transitional leadership. If you are reading this, God wants you to know, IT'S TIME FOR YOU TO LEAD!

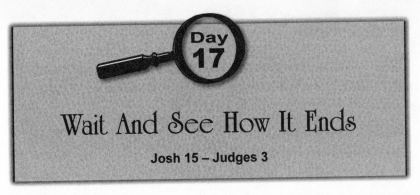

Wait And See How It Ends

Josh 15 – Judges 3

I was watching the final basketball game with baited breath between the Los Angeles Lakers and the Boston Celtics. In the first two games, the Boston Celtics handily dealt with the Lakers to the point of humiliation. Going into game three, if the Lakers had not won, they would have to win the next four in a row — a hefty weight and responsibility for any team to pull off successfully. The momentum and energy was through the roof. In a move that may have been premature as opposed to one of faith, Boston took it upon them to print up: *2008 champions—the Boston Celtics.*

Regrettably for me and a slew of Boston fans, the Lakers squeezed by a win with under 8 points. The print had good intentions but bad timing. Boston assumed it was all over.

How many of us have made bad decisions at the wrong time without giving God the benefit of showing up at the end? The MVP (Most Valued Player) for enduring to the end had to be Joshua. When we look at our reading for today I became antsy on the sidelines. In Chapter 15, there is an allotment for Judah. Chapter 16 speaks of the allotments for Ephraim and Manasseh. Benjamin's allotment is in Chapter 18. In Chapter 19, the allotments for Simeon, Zebulun, Issachar, Asher, Naphtali, Dan and ...finally Joshua!

Here it is; Joshua is the appointed leader, the successor of Moses, mighty in battle, faithful servant, leader of the people and we will not even mention the fact that the book we are reading happens to be named for him! You would think he would get his blessing first or at least in the top five. Not so! God consistently saves the best for last.

Today I want you to take hope in knowing God has not forgotten about you. You may continue to witness other people get blessed and elevated, but go ahead - jump out on faith and print your own T-shirt even before you win that says "Champion: Winning Until The End!"

Me And My Shadow

Judges 4 – Judges 14

Grace, my daughter, made an incredible discovery the other day that I think many of us have come to ignore or take for granted. It was time for her to go to bed and the sun was going down. Frolicking by the window she said, "Look Daddy, I have a shadow." Such simple a statement, yet so profound a revelation. A shadow is the projection of an image that has encountered a bright light, making that image larger than what it is in reality.

When we come to the realization that Jesus Christ is the Light of the world and we were made in His image and likeness, it makes us larger than what we actually are in the natural. Hence, *greater is He that is in us than he that is in the world*. In Psalms 23:4 it boldly declares, "Yea though I walk through the valley of the shadow of death I will fear no evil." In actuality that is a declaration of David to know he can not be afraid of who he is becoming in the Lord for it is much bigger than who he is now. That ought to give all of us a reason to celebrate in knowing you are about to become much BIGGER, STRONGER, AND POWERFUL.

In Judges 9, Gideon's son Abimelech is wickedly evil and ambitious, but through God's grace was still protected. Gaal, the son of Ebed, conspired to take him down and exact a coup. His plan was discovered and Abimelech was warned, so he planned to be proactive and ambush Gaal. Early in the morning when the SUN began to rise, Abimelech's men began coming down the hill. However, there was one problem; the sun hit their image and the enemy thought it was just a shadow. The enemy does not want to believe how much you have grown, matured and developed, but by the time he realizes who you are at the end of these ninety days, he will be defeated.

Keep standing in the Son with study, prayer and fasting and watch how large and in charge you will become!

You Were Too Good For That One!

Judges 4 – Judges 14

I am in Durham, North Carolina this morning for a denominational planning meeting. As I read today's passage, my heart was in two different emotions. One of glee for the victory of the Boston Celtics, and yet another side feeling glum over the predicament of a friend.

As I spoke to a dear friend I had not seen for some time, I asked her the status of her current relationship. She said it ended, as most of them do, because of infidelity! She further lamented that the irony is that they all seem to operate under the banner of Barack Obama's "Audacity of Hope" and insisted on her overlooking the offense and reconcile under a broken heart, broken trust and broken terms. The assailant actually said, "You're not getting any younger, you might as well settle and move in with me."

Here is a young woman who is a disciplined Christian, a devoted prayer warrior, attractive, educated, financially stable and CONFUSED. DO I settle for that ONE or soldier on towards the unknown?

A passage of scripture which captured my full attention is found in Judges 17 and 18. A man by the name of Micah brought silver to his mother, who in turn gave the silver to a silversmith to made false image. Micah then took it upon himself to hire a young Levite to be his private priest. Many people, once they get a little money, prestige and power, think they can deal with the Lord as if He belongs to them alone and no one else. America often deals with the globe on those terms, acting as if the God of Maine does not also have jurisdiction over the Middle East.

In Chapter 18, the children of God were looking for a place to occupy and came upon a parcel of peace, tranquility and productivity, then rationalized it was conquerable. All of us must determine for ourselves that, if in fact we are true children of God, we deserve to have at least a piece of tranquility, peace and productivity in our destiny and in our present. After getting the green light from God to pursue, they went in to claim it and happened upon Micah's private priest (vs 18-19). They told him, "Keep your mouth shut. We are taking you out of here. YOU ARE TOO GOOD TO JUST BE WITH THAT ONE! (I am paraphrasing of course) you should be ministering to a whole nation."

I want to say to someone who is reading this, you have too much anointing, intelligence and focus to be with one who thinks they can control, manipulate and reduce you. Your gift is going to change communities, churches, and cities. The reason why we love the Lord so much is because we know He is way too good for us and to us, but He loves us anyway!

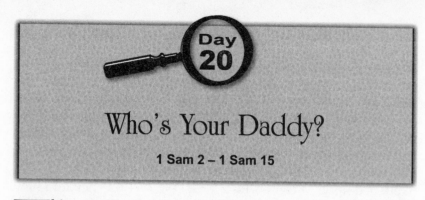

Who's Your Daddy?

1 Sam 2 – 1 Sam 15

This morning I am in Charleston, South Carolina. I was awakened by a phone call that startled and disheartened me at the same time. One of the young zealous members of our church died at 35 years of age. He was a transplant from Minneapolis, Minnesota. While in Minneapolis, he was fully engaged in the street life that ravages so many of our young black men. He became an avid watcher of our television ministry and it highly impacted his life. It touched him in such a way he decided to relocate his entire family to Baltimore in order to become a part of the ministry.

After an extensive autopsy, the coroner still can not find an explanation for his death. His grieving young widow called this morning to see if I would speak to their 5-year-old son who is having a rough time dealing with it because yesterday the neighborhood children began teasing and taunting him. She put him on the phone and I tried to give him a word of encouragement without being Dr. Phil. I asked him how he felt and he responded, "Sad". I asked him whether he missed his dad and he said "Yes". I asked him what he missed the most about his dad and he told me. I told him I would be flying back that evening and if he wanted to talk or hang out, I would be available to him. Before I could hang up the phone, I was prompted to ask him, "Do you know whose going to be your daddy now?" He perked up with curiosity and I told him, "God, because He's been your daddy all along."

I so wish the children of Israel would have had this revelation in I Samuel Chapter 8. Samuel was getting old and his health was starting to fail. His sons had taken on a lifestyle displeasing to God, so Israel asked for a king, not realizing they already had a

God. I hope you know what you have.

I write this morning to every person whose father is deceased; whose father has gone AWOL; whose father does not want to be bothered. I want you to realize who your father is now. Stop looking for a king to replace the void of your father by sleeping with someone for comfort, allowing someone to abuse you or letting someone take advantage of you because you feel like something is missing. You do not know how blessed you are that you have the KING of KINGS and the LORD of LORDS. When Jesus taught the disciples to pray, He did not say, "Address Him as OUR KING," but rather "OUR FATHER."

On this day let the enemy knows WHO YOUR DADDY IS!

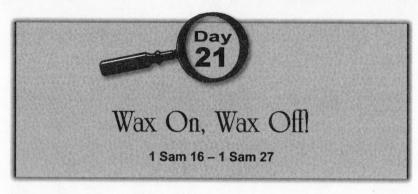

Wax On, Wax Off!

1 Sam 16 – 1 Sam 27

In 1984, there was a movie called the Karate Kid. In this movie, a young man by the name of Daniel and his mother moved from New Jersey to California. After a few weeks in California, he finds out that a dark haired Italian boy with a New Jersey accent does not fit into the blonde hair surfer boy crowd. After a few beat downs from the local boys, Daniel meets a pint-sized gardener by the name of Mr. Myagi who is a martial arts master and agrees to train him. As Daniel begins his training, Mr. Myagi has him doing what appear to be insignificant tasks - painting the fence in precise strokes up and down, waxing the car on with one hand and waxing it off with the other, and washing the windows on the house. Daniel becomes very frustrated because he begins to feel Mr. Myagi's training is useless. He feels he is being trained to be a maid rather than the next martial arts champion as promised. To Daniel's later surprise, it was the small and senseless moves he learned which turned him into the champion at the end of the movie.

In 1 Samuel 16, we are introduced to a young man by the name of David. God had rejected Saul as king over Israel and sent Samuel to find his replacement amongst Jesse's sons. Jesse has a huge dinner and presents his sons, but God rejects them all. Samuel inquired if there are others and Jesse replied, "David." No one thought that God would even consider David as a candidate for king, so they did not send him an invitation to the dinner. How could a ruddy shepherd boy who fed and cleaned the sheep even be considered for the position as king over Israel? What they did not realize is while they were on the battlefield; God was preparing David for destiny. It was David's fight with the bear

32

and the lion that instilled in him the courage to slay Goliath and the strength to lead the king's army. It was during his lone times playing his harp at night under the stars that turned him into a skillful musician. This led him into the king's court , which allowed him to obtain the king's favor. It was during David's time leading and shepherding the sheep he learned how to lead Israel. All of the years he was overlooked birthed in him humility, which allowed him to serve the one he was anointed to replace.

Today, wherever it is God may have you, I pray you do not become discouraged. Everything you are going through is a part of your making. All things work together for the good of those who love the Lord and that are called according to His purpose. You may be on the back side of the desert tending sheep like David, but be encouraged; God has not overlooked you. He is just training you for greatness. Never despise the day of small beginnings; just continue to Wax On and Wax Off. After awhile, you will have all the moves you need to reign in the position God has anointed you for. Remember a king is a king even before he wears a crown.

Cancel The Comeback

1 Sam 28 – 2 Sam 11

I am currently on the train returning home from preaching in New Jersey. My emotions are on a roller coaster regarding last night's game. The Boston Celtics should have clinched the championship against the Los Angeles Lakers since they were ahead in the series. Nobody, including the Lakers based on their performance, thought they had a chance. So now the series continues into Tuesday night when the series should have ended. The Boston Celtics have to live with the reality, and the possibility, of giving their enemies room for a comeback.

In concluding the book of 1st Samuel, one thing jumped out at me which seemed insignificant, but is in fact very poignant. In Chapter 31 after Saul's death, verse 12 states, ". . . and they BURNED his body." The only thing I can think of is they did not want to leave any possibility of Saul having a little Easter and resurrecting. They wanted to insure the evil spirit which kept them bound for so long never reemerged. The Bible declares unto us that in the last days, Satan will be placed in the Lake of Fire. What an awesome stand the children of God have taken to give the enemy no room to make a comeback.

I want to admonish you to absolutely burn away all of your fears, doubt, grief, depression, loneliness, and inadequacy. Do not just bury it because it may come back; instead, if you burn it, it will never resurrect!

Have an incredible day and do not forget to tell all of your past issues to BURN BABY BURN!

Let's Be Unreasonable!!!!

2 Sam 12 – 2 Sam 21

I was in my office this morning trying to complete some much needed administrative work and do the reading at the same time when two things jumped out at me at once. Talk about multi-tasking! I read in 2 Samuel 10:9 where the armies were against David and Joab, both in the front and in the rear. For most of us, this would be an ideal time to quit and surrender. As I was pondering on how they would survive, the following email popped up on my screen. I think it answers the question for all of us as to how to overcome something that seems insurmountable: Be unreasonable.

10 Reasons Unreasonable People Succeed

George Bernard Shaw wrote: "The reasonable man adapts himself to the world. The unreasonable man persists in trying to adapt the world to himself. Therefore all progress depends on the unreasonable man."

It was this view that caused John Elkington and Pamela Hartigan to title their book *The Power of Unreasonable People*. In it, they list the 10 characteristics of successful social enterprise we have found among social entrepreneurs.

Those people:

- Try to shrug off the constraints of ideology or discipline.
- Identify and apply practical solutions to problems, combining innovation, resourcefulness and opportunity.
- Innovate by finding a new product, service or approach to a social problem.

35

- Focus first and foremost on social value creation and, in that spirit, are willing to share their innovations and insights for others to replicate.

- Jump in before ensuring they are fully resourceful.

- Have an unwavering belief in everyone's innate capacity, often regardless of education, to contribute meaningfully to economic and social development.

- Show a dogged determination that pushes them to take risks others would not dare tackle.

- Balance their passion for change with the zeal to measure and monitor impact.

- Have a great deal to teach change-makers in other sectors.

- Display a healthy impatience.

Today in all that you do, if in fact you call yourself a person of faith, you can not just do that which is safe, expected, and the status quo. God is waiting to see how you are going to fight through it all when in the natural there is no way for you to win. People may ridicule, speculate and be confused, but just let them know they are dealing with someone who is reading the Bible in 90 days.

YOU MUST BE UNREASONABLE!

Go For Gold

2 Sam 22 – 1 Kings 7

This morning I am overwhelmed with joy after the Boston Celtics won their 17th NBA title in relentless fashion, trouncing the L.A. Lakers 131-92.

One major thing that kept jumping out at me is the life of Glenn Anton Rivers, commonly referred to as Doc Rivers, the current head coach of Boston Celtics. When interviewed, he said he often thinks about his deceased father, Grady Rivers, who coached his kid's baseball team and proudly watched him become a college star, NBA player and grow into a respected family man. His father gave him important life lessons he uses and relies on to guide the Celtics: patience, being consistent and hard work. Even after his coaching style was criticized and ridiculed for suffering through a horrific previous season, his professional life hanging in balance, always under constant scrutiny from the media, he never gave up. His father's lesson was a powerful motivator for him, as it would be for most of us.

In our passage today, we see David in his final days, teaching his son Solomon life lessons he has relied on to guide his team. (1Kings 2:1). In verse 10, David rested with his fathers and was buried. Solomon now sat on the throne of his father David, and his rule was firmly established.

Most of us are not fighting to win a basketball match on the court, but our struggles are still very real. The problem is, our opponents are sometimes less visible than the game we just watched. We are fighting against our fears, doubts, and the temptation to give up when life becomes too hard. However, if we have a strong goal in mind, something that is vitally important to us - just like the NBA title - we will continue to fight for it. Giving up is simply not an option.

Think about the goals you have had in the past - the ones you did not achieve. Be honest with yourself about why you did not achieve them. Did you give up because you thought the battle was hopeless, or were those goals just not important enough to you? I know some of you still hold your unrealized dreams close to your heart. You have not totally given up on them, but you are no longer actively working toward them. Determine today to reach out for the gold, which is the highest honor. There is somebody else in the world who wishes they had your gift, opportunity and exposure.

Do not worry about "how" you will achieve your goals, no matter how impossible they may seem. The journey of getting there is what is most important. Just lace up those sneakers and dance onto the court, letting your determination shine. It just might be the key that unlocks the door to your hoped for future.

You Never Know!!

1 Kings 8 – 1 Kings 15

I am in the car traveling to Virginia this morning for our annual staff retreat and the Lord brought to my remembrance a testimony from my dear friend, Pastor Zachery Tims in Orlando, Florida. He often recounts how he began his ministry in Florida, having absolutely no roots or ties, just faith. Amidst that faith was a season of enduring financial frustration. He was not sure how to maintain the rent and provide for his family. One day there was a weathered looking Caucasian man in jeans and a polo shirt sitting in the back of his church. Pastor Tims dismissed him as just some vagabond finding his way off the street.

After service the man said, "Pastor I've been assigned by God to help you. How much debt are you in?" Pastor Zach told him and the man paid it all! Pastor Tims to this very day has never seen the man again, but he had to repent because the man did not look the part.

In 1 Kings 13, my attention was captured due to the fact this is a book chronicling the tenures and activities of those in leadership over God's people. In verse 1 however, with no name or physical description, we encounter someone just introduced as 'a man of God'. This man of God had a word of destiny and future, but had no resume or business cards. All he had was a word in his mouth. Be very careful how you treat and handle people. God will assign prophets, messengers and angels along your path who might not look the part but carry out the assignment.

When the man of God in 1 Kings 13 concludes his task, God instructed him not to eat or drink anything while he is there. He turns down one invitation, but the second one he gladly accepts. He embraces the second one because he has been lied to by the host who claims to be a fellow prophet. Immediately after the fellowship, God tears his life away for disobeying His instructions. He himself knew who he was and operated in his gift, but he failed to develop the gift of discernment to evaluate the people he came in contact with.

You must know who you are in God and the gifts that are deposited in you. You must be prayerful about the quality and character of the individuals you let into your space. Angels come disguised as do demons! You never know who God is going to use to bring a tremendous word from on high. You also do not know who Satan is going to use to try to sabotage your assignment. Walk with discretion and anticipating insight.

No Signal

1 Kings 16 – 2 Kings 4

I am in the mountains of Virginia with my staff for a retreat. It is an absolute breathtaking scene, straight from a Norman Rockwell painting. The birds are singing, the air is clean, the locals are riding bikes and the Chesapeake Bay is as placid as one can dream. The staff is motivated and focused to do great things for God in our local assembly called Empowerment Temple. We just have one problem; none of our cell phones have service! We have walked around the resort, stood on the tips of our toes and even one of our global staff members suggested we climb a tree to catch a signal, just as they do in his native country of Uganda. To have no signal means that we have absolutely no communication to call out or to receive incoming calls. This situation has made us value and appreciate what we seemingly have taken for granted, which is living in an environment where we can communicate at will. With exceeding expectation, everybody in a futile manner keeps looking at the phone hoping to see a bar which would indicate a signal.

In I Kings 18, the prophet Elijah is confronting a corrupt king for not serving God. Elijah challenges King Ahab, along with his false prophets, to meet him on top of Mount Carmel for a show down to see who the better carrier was! Who would deliver and who would have a signal - our God or Baal. The followers of Baal kept trying to make a connection and called all day, but to absolutely no avail. The god they served did not respond. Finally it was Elijah's turn to make his call. He sent a message saying, "Hear me, O Lord, hear me that this people may know that You are the Lord God, and that You have turned their hearts back to You again." Within moments fire fell and consumed the burnt sacrifice, the wood, stones, dust and water. Afterwards, Elijah ordered the false prophets of Baal seized and they were later executed. Elijah wanted to show that God was in charge with a sign that there is no other like Him.

I pray the Lord will show you a sign today that He's working in your life and a signal that the enemy will not have the best of your faith!

Healing From Past Hurts

2 Kings 5 – 2 Kings 15

A little over a week ago, golfing phenomena Tiger Woods was able to secure another hallmark victory. His athletic acumen seems to have no bounds as he marches triumphantly towards the record books. In a greater act of marvel moments, after winning the cup he called a press conference. With his baby daughter, Sam, in tow, Tiger announce he would not play for the rest of the season due to an injury in his left leg. What commentators are aghast about is the fact that he had been playing injured for the previous couple of months with a pain that would probably be debilitating for most. The question arose as to whether or not it was ego driven, a business decision or complete lunacy to continue to play with pain that could possibly threaten the rest of his career. There is no question that golf is going to take a hit due to his absence. Viewership and sponsorship always increases when he is on the green. However, the wisdom determinant should be, "Do I sacrifice the season to save a career?" How long was he willing to keep going with pain just to satisfy others?

Most of you reading this have never played golf but you have had a season in your life where you kept going in spite of the pain. Ask yourself today, "Why do I not address the pain of my past? Is it that I do not want others to know? Will it be a signal of weakness? Will the job go on if I need to take some personal days? Is my profession allergic to pain?"

In today's reading, something jumped out at me I want to share with you. The revelation is housed in 2 kings 8:28-29,"he went with Joram the son of Ahab to make war against Hazael king of Syria at Ramoth Gilead; and the Syrians wounded Joram. And

King Joram returned to be healed in Jezreel of the wounds that the Syrians had given him at Ramoth . . ."

Notice my dear friends that it does not make Joram any less to admit he was wounded in a past battle; as a matter of fact when he seeks help they then address him as king. What a noble act of character and courage to know that myroyalty is wrapped in my humility.

Today take some time to reflect on past hurts; not to dwell in depression, but rather to move towards deliverance. Alcoholics Anonymous declares that the first step to recovery is admitting that you have a problem!

I Demand An Appeal!

2 Kings 16 – 2 Kings 25

I recently watched a movie entitled *The Bucket List* were Jack Nicholson and Morgan Freeman star as two terminally ill cancer patients who decide to break out of the hospital and live their last days to the fullest. Edward Cole (Nicholson) is a corporate billionaire who is currently sharing a hospital room with blue collar mechanic Carter Chambers (Freeman).

Though initially the pair seems to have nothing in common, conversation gradually reveals that both men have a long list of goals they wish to accomplish before they kick the bucket, and an unrealized desire to discover what kind of men they really are. Edward and Carter make a break for it. With a checklist that includes: playing the poker tables in Monte Carlo, consuming copious amounts of caviar, racing the fastest machines on four wheels, and much more, these two terminally ill men with only a few months to live do their best to fit a lifetime of experience into their last remaining days. The thing that moved me the most about this movie is that these two men refused to accept their death sentence lying down.

In II Kings 19, King Hezekiah has become deathly ill. The Lord sent a message through the prophet Isaiah, commissioning him to set his house in order for he would surely die. The scripture goes on to say that when he heard this news; King Hezekiah turned his face to the wall and began to weep before the Lord. He reminded God of how faithful he had been and how he pleased Him and walked in His ways. Hezekiah asked God for an appeal (a vindication of a decision) to his sentence. Immediately after he finished praying, God appealed the sentence and sent Isaiah back to Hezekiah. Isaiah told him God heard his prayer and He was

45

adding 15 years to his life.

I am so thankful Hezekiah knew he served the God who was Jehovah-Rapha – 'the God that heals' and the God that is attentive to our cries. Whatever you are facing today that may appear to be dead or dying, remember as long as you have breath in your body, you still have the ability to ask your father for an appeal. Sometimes God wants to see how bold your faith is. Will you just pack up and go home once you have been turned down for the job? Will you stop applying for the mortgage because they denied you once 5 years ago? Will you give up on that son of promise just because he is serving time in jail? Will you throw away the business plan because others said starting it would be impossible? Will you start planning your funeral just because the doctor tells you that he thinks the lump in your body is terminal?

This morning I pray that you will be strong and bold in your faith when you approach life's obstacles. Tear up your Bucket List because it is not over yet. Sometimes God is just waiting to see if you are going to ask for an APPEAL!

Do Or Die

1 Chronicles 1 - 9

Fifty Cents, the world renowned rap artist, a few years ago released a semi-biography cinematic presentation entitled, *"Get Rich or Die Trying."* It describes his meteoric rise from the ashes of poverty to the heights of fame and popularity. He had to make a critical decision in his life as to whether or not he would loathe in self pity and wallow in depression or shake the dust off his feet and pursue his passion and dream. It took a lot of rehabilitation, pain and patience, but through it all he understood that he had but one option and that was to live or die.

The book of 1 Chronicles is the 13th book of the Bible. It contains 29 chapters, 942 verses, 20,369 words, 927 verses of history, 8-1/2 verses of fulfilled prophesy, 7-1/2 verses of unfulfilled prophecy; 30 predictions; 53 commands; 19 questions; 9 promises and 8 messages from God. It appears that Chronicles is mundane and monotonous because it seems as if it is just a litany of people who slept together and procreated; but you must dig deeper to hear and see what God is saying.

For example in Chapter 2 verse 3 it says "...and Er the firstborn of Judah was evil in the eyesight of the Lord and He slew him." The evil thing that caused the Lord to kill Er was not recorded. In the full story as recorded in Genesis 38, we find no further information to assist us. All we know is that it was something God hated so much that it made God kill him. It may have been the same sin that Onan was killed for in Genesis 38:8-10, which was spilling his seed on the ground, refusing to have offspring and reproduce. God commanded man to multiply and replenish the Earth. It is obviously very important to God because this is the first person He ever kills! What a wake up call to know that

God expects you to produce and multiply. This can not be another day of being unproductive. You must produce like your life is on the line! Whatever your dreams, goals, passions, purpose, assignment, drive and ministry are ...DO OR DIE!

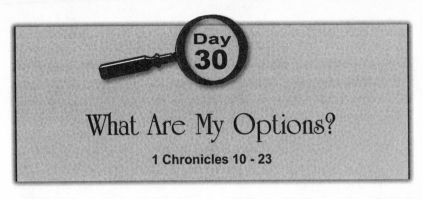

What Are My Options?

1 Chronicles 10 - 23

This morning I am in Birmingham, Alabama at the Full Gospel Baptist Convention. I arose to read a startling article. Much to my amazement it has been reported that one of John McCain's senior advisors has stated that a terrorist attack may very well help their campaign. Using the logic that McCain has a greater record with war, security and global affairs; it would help to his advantage. Even if he thought that to speak it is actually the audacity of insanity. To even infer that losing innocent lives may help push his agenda. Knowing the devastation the nation endured emotionally after 9/11 and the families that were shattered because of it, speaks to the devaluing of life that this Republican has for the nations, citizens, and the troops abroad by which he doesn't mind leaving there for 100 years. What a relief to know we have another option.

In our reading today, we discover in Chapter 21 of I Chronicles Satan incites David to number the troops he has. The reason why the Lord did not want him to hold a census was because they were not his troops. His ego would be affected and he would have been incited to war and not peace once he realized his strength. The Lord was so outraged, he sent disease and death into the land. David immediately began to plead with the Lord for grace. In return, the Lord gave him some options, three years of famine, three months of devastation, or three days of the sword by His hand. David said "I do not want to be in anyone else's hands but yours, because you will have grace." The reality is that he chose the way we should and that is to live as if being in God's hand is the only option!

In verse 14, the Lord killed 70,000 men and had dispatched an angel to wipe out the entire land, but God's grace prevailed. Just before the angel of death was about to execute the nation, David spoke up and said it was not the people who caused this, it was him and asked that the wrath come upon him and not the people. John McCain could assuredly take a page from David's book!

I hope you realize you still have some options without surrendering to defeat! You can choose to finish the next 60 days of reading. You can choose to follow your dreams and passion. You can choose not to allow Satan to terrorize your thinking and your being. Above all choose to live for God like you have no other options!

Time To Pray!!!

1 Chronicles 24 – 2 Chronicles 6

O ne of my spiritual daughters sent me a prayer on Sunday that really impacted me. Sunday was such a phenomenal day of the outpouring of the Holy Spirit that every ounce of virtue was emptied out of me. I barely had enough strength to stand under the weightiness of the anointing.

When I received the prayer, I was encouraged to know someone was thinking about me and lifting up intercession on my behalf. Not an hour after I received the prayer, a mighty prayer warrior of God out of Little Rock, Arkansas called. She left a message proclaiming the incredible move of God she felt at our 11:30 service via Streaming Faith and was compelled to lift me in prayer. I declare there is power in prayer! Imagine my delight in stumbling upon today's reading in 1 Chronicles 29:10-13 where we find David praying before the entire assembly.

10 David praised the LORD in the presence of the whole assembly, saying, "Praise be to you, O LORD, God of our father Israel, from everlasting to everlasting.

11 Yours, O LORD, is the greatness and the power and the glory and the majesty and the splendor, for everything in heaven and earth is yours. Yours, O LORD, is the kingdom; you are exalted as head over all.

12 Wealth and honor come from you; you are the ruler of all things. In your hands are strength and power to exalt and give strength to all.

13 Now, our God, we give you thanks, and praise your glorious name. What a leader to have so much at stake and still take time to pray for the people he's been assigned to lead.

On this the 31st day, I want to pray for you.

Majestic Master and Lord, I come before you today on behalf of the person whose eyes are upon this screen. I want to thank You that you have given them eyes that work. Help them to see that You are moving on their behalf. Let them see TODAY a sign and confirmation that the promise over their life is still fresh. Let them see that their destiny is greater than their down fall. I so appreciate the hands you have given them. Issue renewed strength so they might be able to hold on, carry out their plans and fight like there is no tomorrow. I petition Your Grace to excel their spirit so they might not feel overwhelmed, bombarded, stressed or put upon. Place someone in their way today who needs to rub up against their anointing. If it be Your will do not do it for me, but please answer this prayer because of the ultimate sacrifice at Calvary. I count it done by faith in JESUS NAME, AMEN! I prayed for you, please pray for me. I NEED YOU TO SURVIVE!

Backup Plan

2 Chronicles 7 - 22

Yesterday I was scheduled to leave Baltimore at 11:30 am to travel to Durham, North Carolina for Bishop George Bloomer's regional conference. After being delayed in Birmingham, Alabama, I was behind on some administrative duties and domestic responsibilities which needed my oversight. Given I was not scheduled to preach until 7:30pm, I knew I had some free time on my hands. I contacted my administrator to seek out a later flight so I might tie up some lose ends and still arrive in North Carolina in ample time. Within moments, she called back and said she had found a later flight which would suit my needs. I was appreciative; until I got to the airport that is.

Apparently the later flight was a more popular one, causing it to be oversold. In my original flight I had preferred seating, but in this new adjusted flight I was given a Rosa Parks tribute. The flight was not just crowded but also turbulent. My mind could only wonder how much more peaceful the other flight might have been. But an hour and a half later I reached my destination. It was not the most comfortable, but it met the need.

In the Chronicles reading for today, we encounter the splendid taste of Solomon whereby everything was made of gold. However, in Chapter 12 with great chagrin, we see how Egypt came and invaded Jerusalem and took everything, including the gold shields. King Rehoboam has a resilience we need to adopt. He made bronze spears in their place and carried them proudly. They did not have the shine or 'bling' of gold, but they did the job. What you are driving, where you are working, where you are living and who you are with may not be your gold choice, but bronze is doing the job.

We have been working with our single parents to get them in vehicles commensurate to what they can afford. However, some of their family members did not like the choice because they wanted a Lamborghini, not a Hyundai; however, those who kept there focus understood it was not what is on the outside that matters, but the fact the vehicle will take them where they have never been.

So, whatever state you are in, if the gold has been taken from you, shine up the bronze. You still got it going on!

Who Wants To Be A Millionaire?

2 Chronicles 23 – 34

This morning America woke up in stunned amazement over the rising gas prices. Oil prices climbed to a record above $142 a barrel. It is estimated that the prices could rise well above $150 a barrel this year. Oil is priced in U.S. dollars but the dollar is slipping against key currencies as data shows sluggish economic growth. Analysts are also attributing oil's rapid climb to speculative buying, with traders jumping into the market purely on the expectation that prices will continue to rise.

In 2 Chronicles 25, Amaziah is reigning over Jerusalem and in Vs 9 Then Amaziah said to the man of God, *"But what shall we do about the hundred talents which I have given to the troops of Israel?"* And the man of God answered, *"The LORD is able to give you much more than this."*

God has unlimited resources and the great news is He makes them available to you. In man's economy the law of supply and demand regulates prices. In times of oversupply, the prices go down; in times of shortage, the prices rise. Man's economy fluctuates with the times and seasons; however, God's economy has no shortages. His supply always equals our needs. God does not want you to have any lack, but to increase more and more. As the world depends on buying and selling, God's economy depends on giving and receiving. Whenever you give, you place your self in the position of increase! We can never out give God. No matter what we give to Him, He will multiply it back to us in an amount greater than we gave!

In this time of recession, each Christian in the world needs to be equipped on how to apply what the Bible says about money, wealth, control, needs, generosity, stewardship and contentment in their normal and everyday life. (The Bible has over 2,000 scriptures on money alone!) When we give, God continues to give to us so we could give again. Little wonder Senator Obama and his wife Michelle each gave $2,300, the maximum individual contribution allowed, to the campaign of his former opponent Senator Clinton. Your gift has the power to decide your life circumstances - whether involving financial issues or anything else.

How much money do you want to have? What would you consider to be "enough"? Do you believe you deserve to be comfortable and happy? Once you are clear on what you want, GIVE and it will be so! Give yourself the opportunity of blessing others and you will get powerful! Imagine someone told you they would be sending some money to you, and you knew without a doubt it would be arriving shortly. How would you feel? Feel that way now! There is great power in GIVING! Find somebody or a ministry and give. To plant means to do something and receiving the harvest requires doing something. Our ministry is fertile ground! If there are any billionaires who are reading this and the Lord moves on your heart to bless a poor black preacher, tell me what time you want to meet.

The Hidden Power Of Fasting

2 Chronicles 35 – Ezra 10

A s the exiled Jews prepared to return to Jerusalem, Ezra called for a nationwide fast (Ezra 8:21, 23). *"There, by the Ahava Canal, I proclaimed a fast, so that we might humble ourselves before our God and ask Him for a safe journey for us and our children, with all our possessions ... So we fasted and petitioned our God about this, and He answered our prayer.*

Fasting seems alien to the modern 21st century church. The Bible presents fasting as something that is good, profitable, and expected in our daily walk with God. Fasting and prayer are often linked together (Luke 2:37; 5:33). Although fasting in Scripture is almost always a fasting from food, there are other ways to fast. Anything you can temporarily give up in order to better focus on God can be considered a fast (1 Corinthians 7:1-5).

Fasting is a way to demonstrate to God, and to yourself, that you are serious about your relationship with Him. Fasting is not a way to get God to do what we want. Fasting is a means through which God changes us. Fasting is not a way to appear more spiritual than others. Fasting is to be done in a spirit of humility and a joyful attitude.

It was through prayer and fasting that the early Christians received direction and power from the Holy Spirit for decisions or tasks of special importance.

- Fasting enables us to humble ourselves before God. — 2 Chronicles 7:14, Psalm 69:10

- Fasting is a means by which a believer brings his/her body into subjection. —1 Corinthians 9:27.

- Fasting changes man, not God. God is omnipotent and unchanging.

- Fasting breaks down the barriers in man's carnal nature that stand in the way of the Holy Spirit's omnipotence. — Ephesians 3:20

- Fasting is not a substitute for any other part of God's provision.

- Fasting intensifies prayer and enables the believer to become more effective spiritually. — Daniel 9:2-3; Daniel 10:1-14

- Fasting empowers the believer to obtain deliverance, spiritual breakthroughs, answered prayers, and victory. —2 Chronicles 7:14 - 15, 2Chronicles 20:1-30, Isaiah 58:6

- Fasting prepares the believer to receive a fresh outpouring of the Spirit and the blessings of God. -   Joel 2:12-29

- Fasting has medical benefits. - Isaiah 58:8

This morning I encourage you to fast from anger and hatred, judging others, complaining, bitterness, and spending too much money.

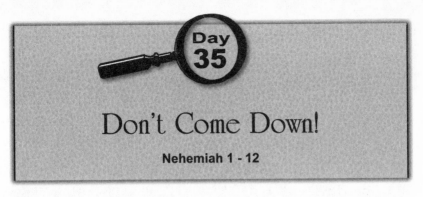

Don't Come Down!

Nehemiah 1 - 12

I recently read an article entitled *"Five Reasons Why People Fail at Achieving Their Goals"* by Nancy East. The first four were very common reasons that anyone could relate to, #1 Not taking Action, #2 Fear, #3 Poor Planning, #4 People's Environment. The fifth one seemed so elementary and common, even though it was stated last on the list. I personally felt it should have been #1 - PEOPLE GIVE UP TO EASILY!!!!

There comes a time when we must learn how to complete our assignment no matter how great the obstacles and oppositions are. You may be faced with debt, low self esteem, lack of support from others or just plain old fear, but the assignment must be completed.

It is during this time that we must learn a great lesson from our reading today in the book of Nehemiah - 'Don't Come Down'. Nehemiah returned to Jerusalem to rebuild the walls which were torn down by Israel's enemies while they were in captivity in Babylon. He rounded up all of the Jews and they began to build. As he started the assignment, he was faced with great opposition from enemies round about (Sanballat, Tobia, Geshem and many more); all trying to convince him to come down and stop the work. They tried several tactics to stop Nehemiah, but he responded *"I am engaged in a GREAT work, so I can't come down"*. Nehemiah made up his mind to do whatever was necessary in order to complete the wall. Half of the men worked while the others stood guard against the enemy. The laborers had a hammer in one hand to build and a sword in the other one to fight. The people worked from sunrise to sunset, never changed clothes and never came down until the wall was complete.

Today, it is time to make up your mind that whatever the enemy may bring your way, you will not come down. No matter how enticing or threatening his attempts are, you must stay on the wall until it is done. When this year began, many of us made great resolutions: lose weight, get out of debt, finish school, start a new business, etc. Even though you have been faced with many obstacles and challenges, I beg you not to come down until the task is completed. If you must cut up your credit cards to get out of debt, stay up all night studying for your college exams, exercise early in the morning to drop a few unwanted pounds or turn off the television and telephone to catch up on your 90-day Bible reading, so be it. Just do not come down.

What if Barack Obama would have come down from the Democratic race when his rivals tried to demolish, undermine and smear his campaign? Where would we be if Dr. King would have come down from the civil rights movement when he was imprisoned and threatened for standing for righteousness? Could you imagine where this world would be if our Lord and King Jesus Christ came down off the cross when His divinity and humanity was mocked and challenged?

It is one thing to start an assignment but it is another thing to persevere and be steadfast until it is completed. As you start this new week, remember the race is not given to the swift and neither is the battle to the strong; but to the one who can endure until the END! So, endure and do not come down until you have finished. Do not give up too easily because the truth is, you are closer to finishing than you think!

Elvis Has Left The Building!

Nehemiah 13 – Job 7

At the birth of rock and roll, the king of the stage was none other than Elvis Presley. He captured America's imagination and directed the energy of its youth. Needless to mention that most of his style and sound was co opted by African American influences, who never even to this day receive their due. His explicit overtures of sexuality were so charged that in a then conservative American market, when he made his television debut they would only show him from the waist up. It was thought his gyrations would appear too controversial. In city after city his concerts were sold out. Taking a page out of James Brown's book at the conclusion of his set, he would feign as if the show was over and then return to make an encore appearance. It became a routine that the concert goers never really knew when the show was over so they would stay anticipating another return from behind the curtain. The promoters, realizing they had a situation on their hands and not wanting to pay late charges, would announce, *"Elvis has left the building"* to disburse the crowd.

In today's reading, we encounter an intriguing man of character by the name of Job. He was a devout believer, a disciplined worshipper and a dutiful father. Job kept all the virtues of God as a priority in his life without being threatened or chastised. We do not see a pastor or prophet breathing down his neck. As a matter of fact, we see his lifestyle not from church, but how he conducted himself at home. He so feared God that he did not just make sacrifices on his own behalf, but also just in case his children fell short. (I encourage you to get my sermon entitled: *JUST IN CASE*)

The plot thickens as Satan enters the scene with absolutely no direction after testifying that he's going up and down looking for something to do. I pray this week you know where you are going and what you want to do. God offers Job as an example to Satan, the one who has been devout, disciplined and dutiful. It goes to show you can do all of the right things and still come under scrutiny. The Lord allowed Satan to touch Job's body, but not his soul. The good news is your stuff does not make you.

Now the good news - Job 1:12 " . . . so Satan left the presence of the Lord."

That is all I want to tell you today, the presence of Satan you faced last week has left! You have nothing between you and your Savior. Stress has left, worry has left, depression has left, guilt has left and shame has left!

What if our Lord and King Jesus Christ came down off the cross when His divinity and humanity were mocked and challenged? It is one thing to start an assignment, but it is quite another to persevere and be steadfast until it is completed. As you start a new day, remember the race is not given to the swift and neither is the battle to the strong, but to the one who can endure until the END! So endure, and do not come down until you have finished. Do not give up too easily because the truth is, you are closer to finishing than you think!

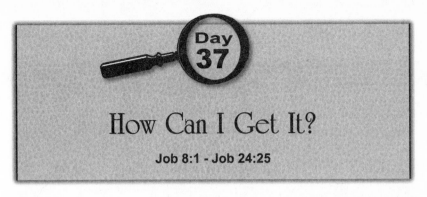

How Can I Get It?

Job 8:1 - Job 24:25

Sunday was one of the proudest moments for me as pastor of Empowerment Temple A.M.E. Church. At our 9:30 service, we issued 50 scholarships to deserving students who want to further their education, anywhere from an associate's degree all the way up to a Ph.D. How my heart warmed to see those fresh out of the prom, all the way to single moms and hard working brothers. I think that is what empowerment should really be all about.

To add ice cream to the cake, several months ago I read an article which said the income of an individual raises by 17% on average if he has access to a vehicle. To that, in conjunction with the Economic Empowerment Committee, we formed partnerships in order to assist single parents who were without transportation. Here is the deal we established - if you are willing to commit to 6-8 weeks of intense training, hold a steady job, and needed a car; at the completion of the course, we would assist you in getting a car and insurance. At the outset, almost 75 registered, but on Sunday 17 focused individuals became certified. At the end of service, I was bombarded by people asking, "How can I get it? I want one. What must I do? When will the next session begin?"

I could not help but think about that this morning while reading the lament of Job. He is pouring out his heart to two of his friends about how he does not understand why life is going so poorly. You can only hope to aspire to get at least two real friends in your life who will be there for you in your darkest hour. What makes the circle of friendship more compelling and attractive is that both of his friends know who the Lord is and believe in His power and strength. In spite of that revelation, Job is troubled by them because they believe it is his fault that he is trapped in the predicament.

Zophar tells him how to turn the curse around in order to get a blessing — a blessing that is not a car, but compassion. In Job 11:13 there are four things Zophar tells Job to do in order to get a blessing:

1) Prepare your heart

2) Stretch forth your hands toward God (verse 13)

3) Put iniquity far from your life (verse 14)

4) Do not let wickedness dwell in your tabernacle (house, life)

If today you are in need of a blessing, not just materially or tangible, but maybe emotionally, spiritually, and physically, I prescribe you take these four and call me in the morning.

Can Not Hold It

Job 25 - Job 41

My 2-year-old twins just started preschool last week. My wife and I were extremely nervous about how they would adjust to going an entire day away from home. Much to our surprise, when we dropped them off, neither of them looked back. Instead, they ran straight to the sandbox, ready to play. We wanted to take pictures of the historic moment, but they refused to stand still and pose. As a matter of fact, the goodbye kisses seemed like that of an awkward teenager in front of their friends at the mall, filled with disgust and shame. The day went through without any incident or accidents.

The next day was a bit different. At midday we received a call from the school notifying us Adore had an accident during play time. When my wife went to pick them up from school, she asked Adore, "Why didn't you tell the teacher you had to use the bathroom? You know better." Adore responded, "I know Mommy. I just couldn't hold it!"

In our reading today we close out the book of Job. Job is closing out his defense unto God about his righteousness and his petition for restoration and clemency for all that he has been through. His friends offer their two cents about their feeling on God's verdict against Job, then emerging from the crowd in Job 32 we are introduced to a young man named Elihu. Its obvious Elihu has been listening to the whole conversation because the text says he burned with anger because of what he heard and could not hold it back another moment. He says in verse 6,"I am young in years and you are aged; therefore I was timid and didn't want to speak." In verse 19, he continues with, "My belly is like wine that has no vent a wineskin ready to burst, I must speak in order to find relief." In other words he was saying, "I can't hold it." Elihu filled six chapters to pour out his opinion and his heart about Job, God and the situation.

Today you must find the voice to speak to the things that have bothered and unnerved you. YOU can not hold it! You must speak to injustice, sexism, poor education and poverty. You must speak up about the things in your life which have offended you so you might move on. The Bible says, "Be ye angry but sin not." You have held it long enough.

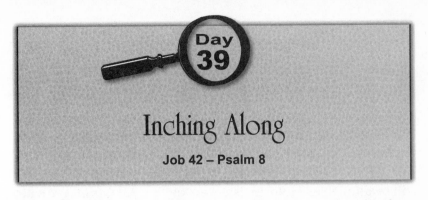

Inching Along

Job 42 – Psalm 8

My three youngest daughters, Grace, Angel and Adore, are at a phase in their lives where they are seeking to affirm their identity. It is not a strange occurrence for them to point out similarities and differences. They are quick to exclaim, "Daddy's the only one who doesn't have on earrings", "Daddy doesn't wear panties; those are for girls", "We're girls, but Daddy's a boy." "Daddy, how come you don't wear berets? Is it because you're not a girl?" All of these are natural in the formative years of understanding your sexuality. However, they do not stop.

Adore likes to be called 'Applesauce', Angel is called 'Banana' and Grace is 'French Fries with Ketchup'. I am no Dr. Phil, but I figure these are foods they like and want to be associated with something that they like. But you guessed it; it does not stop there. The other week we began what all parents dread - the unique art of name calling. That is, moving the naming of one's self to being empowered enough to start naming others. So daily in the car, the house or even in the pool, you hear the never ending declarations akin to Adam in the Garden of Eden, "Adore you're a rabbit," "Grace you're a kitty cat," "Angel you're a birdie." This naming ceremony goes on for what seems like hours. They affectionately call each other animals they know (which maybe all of 12!). It was not until I read this morning's scripture and stumbled upon Psalms 22:6 that it occurred to me nobody called the other one a worm. David declares in this lament, *"I am a worm and not a man!"*

I am sure as David is going over all that is wrong in his present day relationship with the Lord, beginning with raising the question

67

we all have asked, "My God my God why has thou forsaken me?" Then when he called himself a worm, he meant it negatively. Maybe he should have consulted with my daughters and picked another animal, because a worm is not the worst thing in the world to be. A worm can survive in the dirt. A lot of you who are reading this have been in some dirty predicaments but you lived through it. A worm can be placed in a foreign environment and still be attractive. How do fish even know what worms are since worms do not go in the water, but if you put one on a hook, the fish come biting. The anointing on your life is as such. No matter where you go, people are going to come after you. A worm can climb up anything. That is your testimony; you are going to the top of whatever field you might decide. Lastly, I believe people do not want to be identified with worms because they do not move fast; however, it must be said they do make progress, even if there just inching along!

Right now, things in your life might not be going at the speed you would like, but guess what; you are making progress, even if you're just inching along. Thank God for every inch of success, growth and change.

One day at a time, that is all I am asking of you. The reading may seem long, intense and demanding, but keep inching along and you will make it!

Dependence Day

(Rev. Benita Keene)

Psalm 25 – Psalm. 45

The holiday was first observed in Philadelphia on July 8, 1776, at which time the Declaration of Independence was read aloud. City bells rang and bands played. People celebrated with fireworks and candles which they lit and placed in their windows. The first Independence Day celebration took place the following year - July 4, 1777. By the early 1800s, the tradition of parades, picnics, and fireworks was established as the way to celebrate America's birthday. It was declared a legal holiday in 1941.

The Fourth of July is traditionally celebrated publicly with parades and pageants, patriotic speeches, and organized firing of guns and cannons and displays of fireworks. Early in the 20th century, public concern for a safe holiday resulted in restrictions on general use of fireworks. Although fireworks have been banned in most places because of their danger, most towns and cities usually have large firework displays for all to see and enjoy. Family picnics and outings are a feature of private Fourth of July celebrations. Today, the most popular way to celebrate Independence Day is to get together with family and friends, have a cook out and attend a fireworks display.

As I thought about the Declaration of Independence, I thought about a Psalm of David. "Delight thyself also in the Lord; and He shall give thee the desires of thine heart" (Psalm 37:4). At first glance, the words from Psalm 37:4 feel a bit like a blank check. It appears to say, "Enjoy God and get everything you want." But instead of a promise of prosperity, the words are a "proclamation" or a "declaration" of a profound truth; the closer you draw to God, the more your desires will reflect His own. Each verse in

Psalm 37 contains its own unique insight and all the verses work together to convey one important message.

In a recession, Psalm 37 tells you not to worry during times of trouble. This psalm gives your four practical ways to defeat worry when situations seem to get the best of you:

1) Trust in the Lord

2) Commit your way to the Lord

3) Wait on the Lord

4) Delight in the Lord

I look at Independence Day as "Dependence Day." Depend on God to:

- fight your battles

- take care of your family

- provide you with finances

- give you an uninterrupted peace

- fulfill the promise over your life.

As you gather today with family and friends who may be depending on you to pull everything and everybody together; know this - any time you desire something that you know would also delight God, you can depend on Him to give you the desires of your heart.

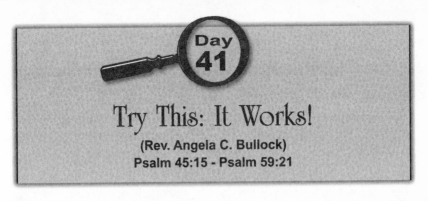

Try This: It Works!
(Rev. Angela C. Bullock)
Psalm 45:15 - Psalm 59:21

It is early morning as I lie upon my bed peering out of the window. It is the dawning of a new day as the light has pierced the darkness and shown forth to the earth. The waters above the firmament are gently streaming down to the earth. Though I am not outside, it is evident the wind is blowing, for the leaves on the trees are swaying. I hear the birds chirping faintly so I open the window. Immediately I feel the warmth in the air and the smell of the morning dew. I realize the breath in my body is in rhythm with the gentle breeze I feel upon my face. I am compelled to break forth in praise, "Like the dew in the morning gently rest upon my heart. Rest Jesus; rest Jesus, gently rest upon my heart."

As I am compelled by the Spirit of God to praise Him, so does the psalmist in our reading for today. The psalmist praises God continually, in good times and bad. The psalmist acknowledges the power, sovereignty, holiness, confrontation, salvation, judgment, and glory of God. In this acknowledgement of all that God is and all that God does, the psalmist declares his trust in God. In God Whose word I praise, in the Lord Whose word I praise – in God I trust; I will not be afraid. What can man do to me? (Psalm 56:10-11)

At a time when nations are in an uproar and kingdoms all over the world are falling, we must declare our trust in God. When the waters above and the waters below the firmament teem to flood and desolate cities, states, provinces, and countries all over the world, we must declare our trust in God. When men boast of evil and lie in the streets waiting to steal and commit murder, we must declare our trust in God. When we live amongst a generation which has rejected God and seeks evil and not good, we must declare our trust in God. When our food supply has been tainted, the price of gas continually rising, and our economic status continually depleting, we must declare our trust in God. When states are making same sex marriage lawful and the divorce rate climbing, we must declare our trust in God. At a time when an African American man can, in spite of all the deceitful tactics and obstacles set in his way, gain the Democratic nomination, there is "Hope for Change" and we must say — "In God I trust!"

We must demonstrate our vows to God and dominate in passing along the heritage of those who fear His name. HALLELUAH!

I challenge you, as you complete your reading for today, go back and write down the first verse of Psalm 46 – 64 and all of Psalm 65. Read this as you lay your head upon your bed and allow your soul to find rest in God alone; knowing that your salvation comes from Him.

Don't Slip

(Min. Christopher Brown)
Psalm 70- Psalm 88

A couple of weeks ago, I was on a staff retreat at one of the most beautifully serene places I have ever been to in my life. For three days, we enjoyed God's creation at its finest. The ocean, the land, and the birds; the entire atmosphere seemed to be just what we needed to refocus, revive and refresh ourselves.

One evening, a few of my colleagues and I decided to take a small boat tour of this place termed as "the east coast's best kept secret." As we sailed along, our captain began showing us wonderfully erected homes worth several million dollars. Each house had a yacht docked on their estate and a pool house as large as somebody's two-bedroom home.

As we continued to cruise along, we saw house after house, yacht after yacht, pool house after pool house, and became even more amazed. What we thought was just a regular boat tour turned out to be something even greater for all of us. Our captain, who we soon deemed as our tour guide, started explaining the disposition of each person who lived in the particular house and told us what they did as an occupation. Although the scenery was great, the boat ride was relaxing and the comradery was appreciated, I could not help but become a little envious of the people who lived in those houses; especially of those whom our captain said were callous and arrogant. I began reflecting on how hard I had been working and some of the long hours I put in, yet I am not living anywhere near how well these people are. The thoughts that kept plaguing my mind [and I am sure some of you have contemplated at one time or another], 'How can somebody who is nasty, or probably not even saved be living this large? It isn't right that we as Christians struggle in this economy, while the rich seem to get even richer with their egotistical and pompous attitudes.'

The writer of Psalm 73 seemingly agreed with my plight that day on the boat when he said in verse 2 and 3, "But as for me, my feet had almost slipped: I had nearly lost my foothold. For I envied the arrogant when I saw the prosperity of the wicked."

In today's reading, we find in this particular psalm the writer makes the wicked, along with their possessions and arrogance, his focus. And because he focuses in on them, he almost slips and losses it. This is a lesson to be learned by all of us - do not make what others have, what others say, or even what others may do your focus. "Don't slip", do not lose your focus! Do not allow the enemy to cause you to lose your concentration on what God has just for you.

If you find that you have slipped, this psalm outlines for us four steps to regain your footing:

- Get into God's presence- for that is where you gain greater understanding (verse 17)

- Allow yourself to be guided by His Word (verse 24)

- Make God your true desire (verse 25)

- Reflect on your past victories, blessings, breakthroughs and miracles and go run and tell somebody! (Verse 28)

The steps of a good man and woman are ordered by the Lord! Don't Slip - Stay focused

Raise Your Hands If You're Sure!

(Min Tessa Couser)
Psalms 89-108

In the late 1980's there was a commercial that sounded the anthem of a popular deodorant called "Sure." The commercial would affirm that if you were sure you are protected, "Raise your hands." People would raise their hands everywhere. The book of Psalms exclaims this anthem, but the homage is not for a deodorant, but for the Only Wise and True Living God.

The Psalmist continually reminds himself God is in control, even amidst chastisement and rebuke. The love and protection of God transcends time and space. There is absolutely nothing which can separate us from the Almighty. Today, you may feel that God is so very far away. It may seem as if He is not hearing you. Even though you pray and cry, God just seems further and further away. Never the less, you continue to remain faithful, but it looks like God got His signals crossed; because as you look around, it seems as if those that mean you harm and have chosen to be your enemies are getting away with so much. You begin to wonder, "What is wrong with me?"

Rest assure my brother and my sister, there is nothing wrong. You seem to have found the door by asking yourself this question. Now, allow me to give you the key to unlock your breakthrough. The Bible declares praise is beautiful for the righteous and God inhabits the praises of His people. There is one common denominator from Psalms 89 to Psalms 108 - praise, worship and trust. As long as you remain in the shelter of the Most High, "He shall give His angels charge over you." (91:11)   God will save and keep you (91:3.)

I remember several years ago, I was going through a major battle.

Like most Christians, I believe God's Word; but at some point in the battle, I started to experience fear. Even though I said I believed, I still became afraid. The Holy Spirit quickly arrested me and said it was not just for me to believe, but to also trust God (I thought they were the same). He showed me I had the basic beliefs covered. As far as Only believing, my preconceived notion of victory would do; but could I still trust God even if I did not appear to win in the natural? I concluded I had no other choice but to trust God, so I put on the whole armor of God (Eph 6) and positioned myself like the Psalmist, to fight this battle with praise, worship and trust. I raised my hands because I was sure that whatever the outcome, God deserved all the honor, glory, dominion and power!

My friend, position yourself today as the Psalmist did in Psalms 103. Command your innermost being to praise and worship the One who forgives all your sins, the One who heals all your diseases, the One who redeems your life from destruction, the One who crowns you with love and compassion, the One who satisfies your desire with good things. I can go on and on, but I would like to declare to you this day to not just raise your hands if you are sure, but "Raise your hands because you are sure!"

Wounded Warrior

(Min. Eva Branch)
Psalm 109- Psalm 134

I wonder: to what extents are you and I wounded warriors? How many of us have hidden wounds known only to ourselves? How many of us are hurting from the after-effects of toxic relationships or dysfunctional families; still recovering from old losses and betrayals; still hearing the echoes of unkind words spoken long ago? How many of us are bruised and broken emotionally, falsely accused, deceived by double-minded people who reside between good and evil, coping with personal trauma, dealing with something very few people, or perhaps no one else, know about? Probably most of us, to one degree or another.

We are constantly being assaulted as we make our way in this world. It is simply not possible to live among other people - in a society, a family, or a church - and not be hurt. That is just the way life is; how it has been ever since Adam and Eve left the Garden, and how it will be until Christ returns. We sin. We wound one another. Sometimes we do it unintentionally, out of ignorance or thoughtlessness. We may not even know when we have done it. Sometimes we do it on purpose, out of anger, pride, or spite. At some point in our lives, we have both caused and experienced pain.

David expressed in Psalm 109: 21-22, "But you, O Sovereign Lord, deal well with me for Your name's sake; out of the goodness of Your love, deliver me. For I am poor and needy, and my heart is wounded within me."

David was a wounded warrior, a man after God's own heart, and he understood how it felt to be in pain and falsely accused. He expresses his concerns to the Lord, asking for help because he was being attacked by evil people who slandered him. Even in the face of his adversary, he remained faithful unto God and continued to show love towards his accusers.

We are called to hate the sin, but love the person. Now lawfully, when we are under attack we must pray earnestly for God to fight our battle, but how many of us would rather set our Christianity on the shelf for a minute and deal with it ourselves? Let us be honest - it hurts to turn the other cheek when you have been wounded with false accusations, especially when you have done nothing to deserve it. The Marines have a slogan that says, and I quote, "Pain is weakness leaving the body." We are all wounded warriors until God releases us from our pain, then He strengthens us with the Holy Spirit so that we can persevere. David was a warrior, a true man of God; and because of his love and respect for God, he had to endure persecution. The same applies to us.

Are you a wounded warrior? Do you need to be healed from your hidden wounds? God is able to heal our wounds and restore our faith. They may be deep and longstanding. They may be a tangled web of confusion and pain, but God sees and understands. Regardless of how sin has scarred us, He can make us whole again.

- He can calm the storm raging in our hearts.
- He can replace bitterness and despair with peace and joy.
- He can rebuild and repair what is broken.

Stay true to God and His word no matter how bad things get. If we keep His words in our hearts and allow it to be a lamp unto our feet, God will provide us with the strength and serenity to overcome any obstacle.

"I Too Know Why The Caged Bird Sings."

(Rev. Melva McGlen) - Psalm 135 – Proverbs 6

Maya Angelou is considered one of the most prolific writers of contemporary literature today. With such works as, *Still I Rise, Phenomenal Woman,* and *I Know Why the Caged Bird Sings.* I can certainly understand why this is the case. She has gained enormous respect around the world for her work and will no doubt be recorded on the pages of history as being a phenomenal woman. Ok, I guess by now you have figured out I am a fan and hope to one day have the pleasure of meeting her.

In her poem *I Know Why the Caged Bird Sings,* Maya Angelou compares the joys of a free bird with that of the plight of a caged bird. Almost immediately, it becomes clear to the reader why the free bird would feel like singing. The world is at its disposal, the sky is the limit, and his opportunities are plenteous. So it is rather expected for him to sing with having such wonderful conditions. In contrast, the caged bird's feet are bound, his wings have been clipped and the bars of the cage have obstructed his view of the sky. Yet he finds reason to sing.

In Psalm 137, the people of Israel were asked by their Babylonian captors to sing a song of Zion. Their response to this request (recorded in verse #4), asks, "How can we sing the Lord's song in a strange land?" This of course arrested my attention.

While there is always a reason to praise God, it is difficult to ignore the arrogance of the oppressor in this verse. In my opinion, this showed total disregard for the plight of their captives. I find it interesting that those who would oppress them would dare ask them to sing; as if the cruelty to which they were being subjected was reason to sing.

This hardly seemed the occasion to request the song of the Lord be sung; however, I do not believe hanging their harps in protest to the oppressor was the best response. The Bible declares,"*The joy of the Lord is your strength.*" (Neh 8:10) This suggests to me there is strength in praising God.

I discovered three reasons a bird sings: 1) when it is content and happy, 2) when it is communicating a message to another bird (including the mating call), and 3) when it is communicating a message to its owner. This discovery opened my eyes to why the caged bird sings.

The caged bird sings, not because he is happy or content. Nor does the caged bird sing because he wants to holler at the cute little birdie perched on the tree outside of his cage. No, the caged bird sings because he needs to get a message to his owner, for he understands it is his owner who holds the key to his deliverance!

So, the next time you find yourself in an oppressive situation, refuse to hold back your praise. Get ready to break free from the oppressor, and like the caged bird, open your mouth and talk to God.

And He hath put a new song in my mouth, even praise unto our God: many shall see it, and fear, and shall trust in the LORD. Psalm 40:3

The poem:

I Know Why the Caged Bird Sings

A free bird leaps on the back of the wind
and floats downstream till the current ends
and dips his wing in the orange suns rays and dares to claim the sky.

But a bird that stalks down his narrow cage
can seldom see through his bars of rage
his wings are clipped and his feet are tied so he opens his throat to sing.

The caged bird sings with a fearful trill
of things unknown but longed for still
and his tune is heard on the distant hill
for the caged bird sings of freedom.

The free bird thinks of another breeze
and the trade winds soft through the sighing trees
and the fat worms waiting on a dawn-bright lawn and he names the
sky his own.

But a caged bird stands on the grave of dreams
his shadow shouts on a nightmare scream
his wings are clipped and his feet are tied so he opens his throat to sing.

The caged bird sings with a fearful trill
of things unknown but longed for still
and his tune is heard on the distant hill
for the caged bird sings of freedom.

(By: Maya Angelou)

The Secret To Success And Happiness

(Rev. Kathy Briggs) - Proverbs 7- Proverbs 20

My favorite author is Og Mandino. I was first introduced to his work by a friend in 1991 who gave to me as a gift a book entitled, *The Greatest Miracle in the World*. This book was given to me right after I had completed an intensive life changing program. Like many, I was looking for people, places and things to make me feel successful and happy. This way of thinking and living caused me much heartache, headache and disappointment. After reading Og's book, I was a fan and bought and read practically everything he had written; however, I missed his book entitled *The Secret to Success and Happiness*. Well, actually I bought the book, but I did not read it; I only browsed through it. Can you believe this? This is what I had been searching for and now the "secret" was being revealed to me in the pages of this book, but I did not read it. They say that insanity is repeating the same thing over and expecting different results. I was insane!

During this time I was also introduced to a prayer entitled the *Serenity Prayer* by Reinhold Niebuhr. In part it says, "Lord grant me the serenity to accept the things I can not change, the courage to change the things I can, and the wisdom to know the difference." That's it! It was not insanity, it was the lack of wisdom. I had been told that "wisdom comes with age". I guess you can imagine how I felt remembering these words. I was no where near old age.

You guessed it, I was miserable. At times I was an outside success and an inside mess, and at other times an outside and inside mess. So you may be asking me why did I not just read Og's book? Well it was not meant for me to read that book. Back then, I did not know, but God knew that I was going to write this article and I needed an eye catcher for a title. Anytime these three words are used either individually or together; secret, success and happiness, it gets the reader's attention.

Now that I have your attention, let me tell you about my favorite book in the Bible. This book is Proverbs; known as the Book of Wisdom. I consider it to be "the real secret to success and happiness." For the past couple of months, all I have been praying for is wisdom; nothing more, nothing less. My assignment, this assignment, is in the book of Proverbs. Be careful what you pray for, you just might get it!

Proverbs addresses how we are to conduct ourselves in every area and aspect of our lives - i.e. spiritually, professionally/business, personally, family, children, heath, romances, finances - every area of our lives. It illustrates the difference between a righteous man and a fool. The chapter of focus highlights two stages of life; the young man and the older man. Although it specifies the male gender, it is also applicable for the female gender.

In 1993, I read *Gifted Hands: The Ben Carson Story*. In it, Dr. Ben Carson, world-renowned pediatric neurosurgeon, states he reads a chapter of Proverbs everyday. He shares that he models his life based on the writings of this book in the Bible, and say reading them has contributed to his personal and professional success.

That is it! The secret to success and happiness is in the book of Proverbs. What a blessing that you do not have to wait to be old to obtain wisdom. Well, that is part of the secret. You will have to read Proverbs for the rest.

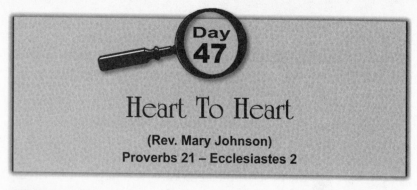

Heart To Heart

(Rev. Mary Johnson)
Proverbs 21 – Ecclesiastes 2

Recently during a family gathering at my mom's place, we were warned upon entering the house that she was having a heart-to-heart discussion with my 17-year-old nephew. The discussion went on for nearly an hour. When he emerged from the kitchen, he had a curious audience glaring at him. Questions were yelled out: "What did she say?" "Did she make you cry?" "How come we didn't hear you talking?" "Are you sad?" He smiled, and said in a gentle voice, "My grandmother loves me!" She says the same thing to me every year: "Listen to your parents, work hard in school, choose your friends wisely and leave those fast little girls alone." We all laughed and the younger brother ran for fear of being the next one to have a heart-to-heart with Grandmother.

In today's lesson, we are bombarded with instructions on how to live our lives for God. Solomon and contributing authors have carefully assembled God's blueprint for righteous living. While reading, I felt so loved by God. There is so much passion as we are guided through what God's expectations are. There is not an issue dealing with life which is omitted. Proverbs 22:17-19 explains how to understand the Words of wisdom.

17 Pay attention and listen to the sayings of the wise; apply your heart to what I teach;

18 for it is pleasing when you keep them in your heart; and have all of them ready on your lips,

19 So that your trust may be in the Lord, I teach you today.

God truly has a heart for us. Enjoy your heart to heart with God as you continue your journey through the Bible in 90 days.

Where's Your Heart?

(Rev. James Turner II)
Ecclesiastes 3- Song of Solomon 8

As we are in this season of recession and transition, we are reevaluating our lifestyle of spending, adjustments, and faith. I had to bury my grandmother last week and as I look at these two books, it brings comfort to my soul. Ecclesiastes brings peace for the future. The author lets us know how to handle life's ups and down.

In Chapter 3 of Ecclesiastes, Solomon shares with us the different emotions we have to endure during the journey. Not only that, but in Chapter 9, he gives us guidance as to how to put life in perspective. After you know what to expect in life, now it is time to enjoy it. Enjoy family, nature, friends, success, dreams to reality, and God.

In Song of Solomon, we transition to the wisdom of love. What passion there is coming from the heart of Solomon. One will interpret these songs as religious, romantic, secular love, marriage liturgy, and poetry. God is not even mentioned in this whole book. But it should show how to love and what love is in several areas.

There is something I want to focus on in this book. In Chapters 3 and 5, the text talks about a nighttime search. This is what love is. Dealing with the matters of the heart, whether a business, spouse, ministry, or God, my heart and my love for something goes all over at night to search what my heart desires. How our life will be better, how our business will grow, how our relationship with Christ will be so much stronger if my heart will drive me to look for my destiny at night.

The question is, what do you love? And what do you love that keeps you up at night? Does it align with the purpose and will of God?

It's Time For Inventory!!!!

Isaiah 1 – Isaiah 12

This weekend I spoke to a very dear friend of mine who I attended school with. We have been friends for quite some time, but rarely get a chance to hang out. Since I had a very long week on me, I phoned him and asked if he wanted to grab a bite to eat and catch up on a few things. He responded "I would love to, but I don't get off of work until 2:00 a.m."

I was taken back by his response because I know he is one of the regional managers for Neiman Marcus. I also know the store closes at 9:30 p.m. daily. I began to question and he replied it was INVENTORY TIME. It is the time of year the store stays open after hours and every employee must stay behind to participate in this process. As the sales quarters change, employees must make a detailed list of everything that is in the store, everything that was sold and everything that is missing.

Today we start the book of Isaiah. This book involves the ministry of one of God's great prophets, who lived in the latter half of the 8th century before Christ. He prophesied for a period lasting forty to sixty years during the reigns of four rulers of the southern kingdom of Judah: Uzziah, Jotham, Ahaz, and Hezekiah.

The kingdom of Judah was in a state of spiritual decline. Religious superficiality and rampant immorality saturated the countryside. The nation had ceased to trust in God and was inclined to form protective alliances with certain pagan powers (Assyria to the east and Egypt to the south). Isaiah's task was to proclaim to them the Lord's word, affirming that security is grounded in the one true God, not in powers of the world. He commands the people to take an inventory of their lives, turn from their wicked ways, tear down their idols and cease from rebellion; otherwise the judgment of God would begin. For all those who would turn and trust in Jehovah again, he promised them hope and safety in the arrival of a Messiah, 'Jesus Christ'.

In this day and age, I know we have begun to preach a gospel full of blessings, prosperity, free of challenges and full of mercy. But we must remember we also serve a God of judgment. My desire for all of us today is we will take a personal inventory of our own lives and see where we stand with God. Are we still being faithful to his commands? Are we still walking upright before Him and doing our best to serve Him in every area of our life? No matter where your inventory is today, whether it's high or low, be encouraged. Rejoice and remember in Chapters 7, 9 and 11, Isaiah predicted a Savior, A Wonderful Counselor, A Mighty God, an Everlasting Father and a Prince of Peace - Jesus Christ. Take heart! His strength is made perfect in all of our weaknesses and He gives us the strength to overcome every obstacle; however it is our responsibility to take inventory of ourselves. The first step to receiving help is to know and admit that you need it.

Your Reservation Has Just Been Cancelled

Isaiah 14 – Isaiah 28

I want to start today by thanking in a real way my ministerial staff who stood up to the plate last week while I was away at my national convention for the African Methodist Episcopal Church. It has been a week like you cannot imagine.

My father was elevated as the presiding Bishop and I served as the campaign manager for Reverend Ann Lighner Fuller to become a bishop. Both of those entities kept me running from 6 a.m. to 1 a.m., leaving me five hours of sleep a night. It started last Thursday and ended this past Friday. I flew home last Saturday night to preach at all three of our services, spend a couple of hours with my family and then flew right back.

By Tuesday I had hit a wall and my whole body was sore. I had calluses on my hands and feet and felt like there was no way that I could continue at this pace. My staff booked me an appointment at the spa for 1:30 on Wednesday, but the business session ran over and I arrived 40 minutes late. The receptionist greeted me with a smile and kindly told me that because of my tardiness, the "appointment has been canceled." I tried to explain how bad I needed it and the kind of week I had, but there was no relief in sight because the books were completely full.

The children of God have been campaigning since we left them in the book of Exodus coming out of the Red Sea. They go through the book of Joshua into the Promised Land. They have to live through a series of bad kings and corrupt priests, as well as depressed prophets. They learn how to sing the Lord's song in a strange land. They witnessed the Ark of the Covenant being taken from them and then returned. They sing through 150 Psalms and get

31 chapters of wisdom and finally arrive into the book of Isaiah. They have to be tired.

The Lord is gracious enough to see their grief and gives them an prescription for their pain. In Chapter 16, Moab is promised ruin. In chapter 17, Damascus can not stand. In Chapter 18, Cush is crushed. In Chapter 19, Egypt is annihilated. In Chapter 21, Babylon is beaten, and in Chapter 23, Tarshish is trampled. Finally in Chapter 28, the appointment for their demise is canceled in verse 18. *"Then your covenant with death will be annulled and your agreement with hell will not stand!"*

I am here to tell you God sees how tired you are of running, fighting and just existing. He sent me back from Saint Louis to tell you, your appointment with death, disease, depression and debt has just been canceled. The enemy waited too late to get you!

No weapon formed against you shall be able to prosper!

How Did You Get In There?

Isaiah 29 – Isaiah 40

D uring my college days at Morehouse College in Atlanta, Georgia, I ran with a group of guys who had a knack for the innovative and the unconventional (to put it mildly). We were focused and determined to not be denied entrance into any event or gathering that was worth attending. For the sake of anonymity and safety, the names will be withheld until the rapture.

There was one particular party we wanted to get into, but only one of us had the money to get into it. So, we gave that ticket to an attractive young lady from Spellman, along with a huge duffle bag. Then we went to the print shop and printed up black t-shirts with yellow ink that said 'SECURITY'. Once inside, we found our 'ambassador' with the duffle bag and switched t-shirts.

On another occasion, the college was having a $1,000-a-plate fund raiser for the school's endowment. Hosting such heavyweight alumnus as Spike Lee, Samuel Jackson and even an Olympic gold medalist Edwin Moses, the dean walked up to us knowing we were all struggling college students and asked, "How did you all get in here?" We all looked dumbfounded but finessed enough to change the subject.

My mind went back to these forgotten moments this morning while I was doing the reading because something captured my attention. I am not sure I ever noticed before in Isaiah Chapter 37 where Rabshaken is continuing his speech to try and break the faith of the believers as he attempted to do in Chapter 36. Please know this, the enemy is all talk. He will do whatever possible to throw you off your game by getting in your ear and reminding you of all your failures, but never bringing up your victories. He runs down the litany of all the nations that did not survive warfare. Then in Verse 12, he says something we have not heard since Genesis, "What about the people in Eden?" EDEN! I did not know anybody lived there since Adam and Eve were kicked out and a flaming sword put at the entrance.

There must have been a group of people who found a way to break back into a place where they had no business. Eden is the place of God's presence and power. Today I want you to find a way to break into the presence of God. Fast today if you must, worship while in your car. Start singing for no reason! Lift up holy hands randomly! Get so close into His presence the angels will have to ask, "How did you get here!"

Much emphasis, thought and consideration are often given as to how the Lord chose Mary to be the mother of Jesus. She had to have been pure, focused and disciplined. Outside of a men's day service or in the midst of the Christmas season does anybody ever mention why Joseph was selected. Outside of his noble character and faith, I want to suggest to you I believe forthrightly that God leaned towards Joseph because of his profession. That's right, a carpenter. Why is that so significant you might ask? We live in the post industrial age, in a technological world. Very few of us push our children to go into carpentry. While that might be true when one studies the Word, it is easy to discover how the Majestic One has an affinity for trees.

In Genesis 3:8, we find a man behind a tree. Adam and Eve had just fallen into sin by eating of the forbidden fruit as offered by the serpent. Hearing God move through the garden, they looked for a place to hide and somehow or another believed that a tree was a good place to hide. The irony is they were hiding behind the very entity God pointed out to them as the focal point of the garden where there were TREES of good and evil.

In Genesis 6:14, we find a man in a tree. The Lord was completely disgusted with man because of their sinful ways and took it upon himself to wipe out the earth because of regret. Before doing so, he remembered Noah and gave his family a way of escape. The first call of order to prepare the ark was to go cut down some trees. He needed a tree to escape.

In 1 Kings 19:4, we find a man under a tree. Elijah had just finished the greatest victory of his life; wiping out the false prophets of

Baal. Hearing the news, Jezebel threatened to take Elijah's life. The prophet slipped into depression and sat down under a tree lamenting his life, until the angel of God came and encouraged his heart.

In Luke 19:1-6, we find a man up a tree. Zacheas was a tax collector, short in stature, who heard Jesus was coming to town. He climbed up a sycamore for a better look. Jesus came straight to the base of the tree and asked him to come down and take Him to his home to share dinner.

In Acts 5:30, we find a man on a tree. Jesus died for our sins, not by lethal injection or an electric chair, but rather on a tree. Coincidence? I do not think so!

In our reading today, Isaiah 41:19 says, "I will plant in the wilderness the cedar, the shittah tree and the myrtle and the oil tree; I will set in the desert the fir tree and the pine tree and the box tree together."

The Lord must really like trees. Much of the environment is in peril today because of the absence of trees. Conservationist and environmentalist are scarily trying to plant more trees. It affects the ozone layer, oxygen and humanity.

Your spiritual assignment today is whenever you pass a tree, lift a word of prayer, offer a praise of thanksgiving, or meditate on the awesome strength of our God.

When Is Image Everything?

Isaiah 52:13 – Isaiah 66:18

Ralph Waldo Emerson, considered one of the great orators of the time said, "What lies behind us and what lies before us are tiny matters compared to what lies within us." While what has happened in the past and the preparations of the future do affect us, the most important is what you do with your gift. We live in a time were people will judge you for what you drive, what you wear, the square footage of your house, the phone you carry and who you know. The concept of image being everything is not new, but resonates with our culture like never before. The question to ask is: "When you look in the mirror these days, how satisfied are you with what you see?"

I believe what lies behind me has had a great impact on the person I have become today. In our passage today, eight centuries before the arrival of Christ, the prophet Isaiah stood in chapter 53:2 and spoke of Christ's humbling image. "He grew up before him like a tender shoot, and like a root out of dry ground. He had no beauty or majesty to attract us to him, nothing in his appearance that we should desire him."

Jesus did not start off His life or ministry like one would expect for someone sent from heaven. He is described as a tender shoot out of some dry ground rather than some majestic tree. A shoot is just a sprout or beginning of life. One can step on it and crush it without even knowing it. Without water, the sprout is all the more vulnerable to be broken off. He was born in a little unknown town of Bethlehem in dingy circumstances (stable). There was nothing particularly impressive about Him. His beginning was so terrible and horrible yet his ending was magnificent. He should have been treated royally, but came as a peasant.

His success had nothing to do with His physical features, good looks, education, wealth or status. But God's gift is what He really needed. Our success is not rooted in who we are but how much Christ lives within us. Do not despise your weaknesses because that is where God wants to show more of His glory and strength. "He was despised and forsaken of men, A man of sorrows, and acquainted with grief. And like one from whom men hide their face, He was despised, and we did not esteem Him." (Isaiah 53:3)

I can only imagine the fact God made mankind to be sociable, kind and accepting, but His Son had none of these things surrounding His birth. He was not only persecuted from His birth upwards, but also socially rejected by those who should have learned from Him.

Maybe you come from a broken, dysfunctional home; you've been an alcoholic or branded an 'ex'. Maybe your childhood situations where so horrible, no child should have to go through it. I came to encourage you - what lies behind you is history, but what lies ahead of you is a lifetime of discoveries, wonders, dreams and possibilities. The key to unlock them is the gift that lies within you. You are gifted to make a difference, save someone's life, write a book, marry and live the kind of life you have dreamed. Today, seize life and make the best out of it. Do not wait for tomorrow!

Take all your mistakes and learn from them. Chose to overcome the imperfect situations and use them to your advantage. Your past or future does not matter as much as what you have inside of you at this moment.

Prenatal Care

Isaiah 66 – Jeremiah 9

I am sitting in the Atlanta Airport on a layover from the Bahamas, heading to Denver, Colorado. Sitting adjacent from me is a pregnant mother who seems to be in the last stretch of her journey. She has taken her shoes off due to obvious swelling. Her husband has darted off to get her something to eat since she is eating for two. She must get prepared for our 4 hour flight in the air to Denver. She is reading the New York Times best seller, *"What to Expect While Expecting."*

I pray silently for the child's future and destiny, believing by faith the child will go to the top of whatever field he/she chooses and the child will always be centered in the love of the Lord. I think to myself this baby has no idea how many x-rays have been performed to monitor her/his growth, how many shots have been injected to add nutrients to their system, how many activities avoided to insure their safety, how many smoke filled rooms were passed to block the smoke, how many drinks were not consumed so as to avoid contaminating the child's equilibrium.

You might ask why I am giving so much thought to a pregnant mother I do not know and a child I have no connection to. Well, the reason is because I have just finished reading our chapters for the day and I can not shake my spirit off Jeremiah 1:5, "Before I formed you in the womb I knew you; Before you were born I consecrated you; I appointed you a prophet to the nations." I am mesmerized considering what kind of prenatal care the Lord did for us!. Just to know that before your father's sperm reached your mother's egg, God had a plan for your life. It is mind boggling to know while you and I were still in our mother's womb; He already picked our purpose and profession. With that in mind, there are some things God had to put in us from the time of the womb.

You could not have been aborted or miscarried because God knew what you were going to become. He shielded your mother from certain environments just to protect you. He instilled a diet of faith, courage and strength to equip you for battles you did not yet know about. He gave you shots of determination and perseverance. Have you considered how you have been able to endure certain things that would have killed other people? They do not understand you were born with a certain tenacity the world can not shake.

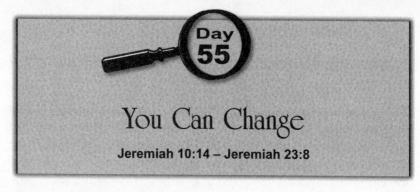

You Can Change

Jeremiah 10:14 – Jeremiah 23:8

L ast night I preached in Denver, Colorado for a family conference. When the service was over, a reception was held to welcome me to the city. Amongst the guests, I was privileged to meet a woman who is an addiction therapist. She happens to also be an ordained minister.

She began to lament on how taxing her job can be because her agency provides all the tools necessary for anyone who wants to be delivered from substance abuse, but so many times the people who they service end up coming back into the program from a relapse. They offer job training, housing placement, educational opportunities, financial literacy, spiritual direction and support groups. In a sigh of release, she finally exclaimed, "It's not until the client has a change of mind that they will ever be free."

In today's reading, Jeremiah is operating as a therapist and a weeping prophet. He knows they have the potential to be better as the chosen children of God, but they keep going back to false gods and idol worship. He is frustrated because the Lord keeps giving them chance after chance, yet they refuse to hold fast to their covenant. The wrath of the Lord is about to be exacted, but it can be derailed if they would only change. In Jeremiah 13:23, he says, *"Can the Ethiopian change his skin or the leopard his spots? Then also you can do good who are accustomed to do evil"*. He believes in their ability not to adapt, but rather to change. Many of us adapt to the environment we are in, but never really experience change. Whatever you have been doing, *you can change!*

You can stop smoking! You can stop drinking! You can stop having a temper! You can stop overeating and overspending! You can stop being a gossiper. You can stop internet pornography and addiction to chat rooms. You can change! Try to today!

If God put so much emphasis on nurturing and developing you in the womb, please do not think He's not doing a work right now! Do not suffer from postpartum depression; its going to be better!

It's Good For You!!!!

Jeremiah 23:9 – Jeremiah 33:22

A friend of mine had his first encounter with the amazing healing power of castor oil during a business trip to Amsterdam, Holland nearly 4 years ago. As he got off the plane from Toronto, he felt a sharp pain in his lower back, radiating down into the leg. Whether it was triggered by the long hours of sitting crunched up in an uncomfortable airplane seat or by the heavy suitcase he carried, he will never know. By the time he arrived at his hotel room, he was in agony, barely able to stand up straight. Even lying down on the bed was painful.

What was he to do? He did not know anyone in the city and was scheduled to attend some important meetings the following day. The staff at the hotel's reception desk could not tell him how to locate a chiropractor. He was not interested in going to a doctor for a prescription painkiller or muscle-relaxant. He remembered his grandmother had often suggested castor oil packs for various aches and pains, and remembered having read of its effectiveness in cases of sciatica.

He managed to take a cab to a nearby drugstore, where he purchased a bottle of castor oil. No doubt the pharmacist thought my friend was bent over because of constipation. The pharmacist handed him the small brown bottle and said these words "Once it starts working, it may not feel good to you, but it's good for you."

The prophet Jeremiah had a most difficult message to deliver. Jeremiah loved Judah, but he loved God much more. As painful as it was for Jeremiah to deliver a consistent message of judgment, Jeremiah was obedient to what God told him to do and say. He is taunted, put in jail, at one point thrown in a pit to die. He was often bitter about his experience and expresses the anger and frustration he feels. He is not depicted as a man of iron, and yet he continues in preaching and praying for God's people. Jeremiah hoped and prayed for mercy from God for Judah, but more so trusted that God was good, just, and righteous.

We too must obey God, even when it is difficult. We must recognize God's will as more important than our own desires. There are times when the will of God will cost you friends, money, fame and self-satisfaction, but you must be confident and be willing to persevere through everything. Like the Prophet Jeremiah, you may feel rejected, alone, unsure and sometimes depressed, but you must have confidence in the One who has sent you.

In Jeremiah 29, God promises, *"For I know the thoughts that I think toward you,"* saith the LORD, *"thoughts of peace, and not of evil, to give you an expected end."* I pray that whatever the will of God is for your life, you will have the courage, discipline and confidence to walk in it today, no matter what the circumstances are. You can acquire great riches, a wonderful career, a beautiful home and the prestige and praise of countless of individuals, but if you are not in the complete will of God, it all means nothing. It is in His will that you will find peace in the midst of turmoil, comfort in the midst of despair, and hope in the midst of all of your fears and joy even in times of sorrow.

It may appear right now as if your life is going crazy, everything is in complete disarray and you may not even know your next move. Rest assured, as long as you are in the middle of God's will, everything will work out for your good because God has an expected end for you. The will of God may not feel good to you, but it is always good for you!

Burn Baby Burn

Jeremiah 33:23 – Jeremiah 47:7

Our church was so privileged yesterday to have CNN visit us for worship. They came to interview some of our members as part of their special airing this week entitled *Black in America.*

Regrettably I have not had a chance to see it as yet, but I hope one of the slices of black history they bring up is when Dr. Martin Luther King Jr. was assassinated and the riots that ensued across the country; most notably the riots in Watts, California.

The city was enraged and as a consequence, set ablaze because the youth were unsure how to channel their frustration. It was an act of defiance, rebellion and discord. As the National Guard was brought in to restore order, there was a chant which could be heard from the city, "Burn baby burn!" A few days later, a haze of smoke was in the air as a reminder of what occurred. Looted businesses were ransacked, and the police were ever present, but the pain of the people was only rivaled by their resilience to soldier on.

In our reading this morning, I was held captive for a long time in Jeremiah 36. Some of the things which jumped off the page I want to share with you. First of all in verse 5 where Jeremiah calls for Baruch and tells him, *"I've been banned from coming to the church."* A lot of people are on self imposed exile from ministry. They can go, but because of incidents and accidents, they do not feel comfortable. Whatever has happened, do not let the enemy stop you from going to church!

Jeremiah then gives him a scroll and tells him to start taking dictation. The Bible says *"Write the vision and make it plain . . .*

though it tarry wait on it, and it shall come to pass." Habakkuk 2:3. Thus reading the Bible in 90 days has helped me immensely, not just the Word, but writing notes. It has been cathartic and developmental. During the Dream series, I encouraged all of you to get a journal, start writing what you hear God saying, what you dream, what you think and how you feel.

Baruch wrote down everything as he was instructed and brought it to the church house where it was read. The priests were so moved; they said the king needed to hear it. The strength of writing is that your work will go where you never can. (I am challenging those of you who have a book in you! Stop playing; you know it is in you.) The priest then took it to the king, but because God knew there would be an attack, He hid them (vs. 26). If you cultivate your gift, talent and purpose, God will hide you from attack! The king did not want to receive it so he began to burn the pages from the scroll after reading it. The good news is the story does not stop there. In verse 32, Jeremiah took another scroll and dictates again!

Tell the enemy, BURN BABY BURN! Whatever he thinks he has destroyed, God is going to give you the power to develop it again, create it again and produce it again!

Man Up

Jeremiah 48:1 – Lamentations 1:22

Yesterday the thrust of my devotion focused on rebuilding after the enemy burns up your work, effort, and productivity. It also encouraged you the reader to take on the discipline of reading. As a sidebar, I mentioned CNN came to the church to do some auxiliary work and interviews for their special, Being Black in America. One church member took us into a place of introspection and challenge as to how we must break our own limitations and assess the exceptions to the stereotypical rules placed before us. The church ought to be the place to examine the issue at length and give, not just critique, but some direction as to how we proceed. It is noteworthy to mention that Soledad Obrien, amidst her research on the special, had to do a second day just to focus on the state of black men.

We have heard the statistics time and time again. There are more black men in jail than in college. More than 50% of our black men are on drugs, incarcerated, on parole, homeless, suffering mental illness, living with HIV or homosexual. Most of our churches are 70% female and 60% of our homes are female led. Black women are leading in businesses, finance, education and spirituality. Just in writing this, I feel like Jeremiah, the weeping prophet. As in the early account of Genesis after the fall of Adam and Eve, I want to ask, "Adam where are you?" What has happened to our brothers? Where are our men?

I rose at 5:45 this morning to do my morning devotion and today's reading. Amidst study I stumbled on Jeremiah 50 where the Lord laid out the blueprint for exacting revenge on the Babylonians for what they did to the children of Israel and the children of Judah (verse 33-38). I was on the edge of my bed, captivated by every word, but startled when I got to verse 37. A sword against her horses and against her chariots and against all the foreign troops in her midst, that they may BECOME WOMEN! WHOA!!!! He said he's going to make the men not become LIKE women but become women. My head is spinning, does he mean he's changing their gender, their role, their position, does it mean he's shifting the power?

I see two things in this. One is that women in the absence of strong men are going to take the responsibility of men as they have been doing; serving as both mother and father, provider, warrior, leader, defenders of the community and priest of the home. I also see that our brothers need to MAN UP and stop crying "Whoa is me!" Jeremiah was beaten, sent to jail, separated from his family and ostracized; but still fulfilled his purpose. He did his job and died for the cause. God is looking for a few good men (and women)

I guess it is only appropriate to go to lamentations and cry it out before we bring it all together!

You Are What You Eat

Lamentations 2 – Ezekiel 11

I remember vividly growing up and watching cartoons every Saturday morning. In between cartoons, they used to have little vignettes to help young children develop, grow strong and become model human beings. Little messages about not talking to strangers, looking both ways before you cross the street, the value of sharing and the benefits of reading.

One of my favorites was a presentation entitled; *You are What You Eat!* If you eat a lot of candy, you would have an excessive amount of energy but insufficient protein. If you drank milk instead of soda, you would grow tall as opposed to rotting your teeth out. If you had fruits and vegetables, your heart, blood and mind would be able to operate in tip top shape. As it is in the natural so it is in the spiritual.

Those who watch a lot of horror movies are prone to live on the edge because they have eaten a diet of fear and risk. Those who intake pornography are more accessible to sexual expression because they have eaten that. Those who are surrounded by profanity in regularity do not think twice about what language they use because of the environment they are steeped in. The same can be said in terms of your spiritual diet.

If you are in a ministry with a lot of candy and soda, but no protein, vitamins or meat; you will produce a sound with a lot of shouting and expression, but no growth or development. You must have some meat. That is why these 90 days of reading the Bible are going to help foster your growth by leaps and bounds.

In Ezekiel Chapter 3, the Lord makes this principal praxis. He says in verse 1, "Son of man, eat whatever you find here; eat this scroll, and go, speak to the house of Israel." Verse 10 of Chapter 2 tells us the ingredients, or the recipe, in the scroll, ". . . *and there were written on it words of lamentation and mourning and woe."*

We have just concluded reading Jeremiah and Lamentations, so we know intimately well what the prophet wept about and lamented over. The children of Israel and Judah had forsaken the ways of God and were facing utter annihilation. God has now raised a new leader who can try to speak sense into His people since they would not heed the call of Jeremiah with any real consistency. God told Ezekiel, *"When you finish eating the word, than I charge you to go and speak what you have eaten."*

What is in your diet? What are you speaking? In these days of reading the Bible, your speech should have changed. Can people hear anything different in your voice? Are you feeding your faith and starving your fears? Today I challenge you to talk to somebody about what you have read from the Word of the Lord and see what difference a diet of the Word can make.

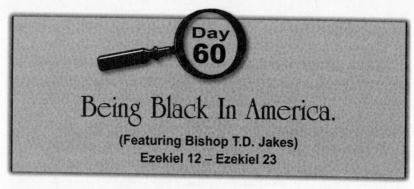

Being Black In America.

(Featuring Bishop T.D. Jakes)
Ezekiel 12 – Ezekiel 23

I am in Detroit this morning, preparing to fly to Connecticut. The service in which I was blessed to minister in had a supernatural move of God where countless hundreds of people were baptized in the Holy Spirit. I rushed back to my hotel to try and get a piece of the CNN special, *Being Black In America*. Much to my dismay, it had already concluded. I scoured the Internet to no avail trying to find snippets, but none have surfaced yet. I did stumble upon an article written by my mentor, Bishop T.D. Jakes, that so riveted me I wanted to share it with you.

Bishop T.D. Jakes

Senior Pastor, The Potter's House

I am delighted to see a continued rational discussion about race relations in this country. I know many find it painful and some would rather not discuss it at all. But like a good marriage, sometimes communication is the only way to create unification. Therefore, I applaud CNN for having the foresight to lead a discussion that hopefully will produce more love and a shared concern for people you see every day, but might not know what they see when they live in the same world and breathe the same air that you do.

Often I pen words as a pastor, sometimes as an entrepreneur, and occasionally as a citizen with an opinion. But today, I have been asked to share a story as a father and a person of color, who knows firsthand the challenges of raising children of color.

I love this country and I am very proud to be

an American. In spite of its many challenges and disappointments, I fervently believe that the benefits of living in the United States ultimately outweigh the liabilities. But in the interest of sharing a "what is it like to be you" story, I will add this one to the discussion. To be sure, we are not all monolithic. Many, many blacks have raised their children surrounded by masses of blacks and have faced a different challenge than mine.

I have twin boys who are almost 30 years old now. But when they were very young, I was sitting with both of them in the predominantly white environment of my home in West Virginia talking about things fathers discuss with their sons. I shared with one of my sons that when I was his age my skin tone was very much like his, very light. In a matter of fact way, I mentioned that as I got older, my skin darkened and changed to become much more like his brother's skin, which was darker.

My son, whose skin tone was lighter, began to cry profusely. I was befuddled by his reaction, but when your 7-year-old is crying without a reason and you love him, you investigate it immediately! So I asked him why he was crying. He blurted out, "I don't want to get blacker, Daddy!" He looked at me in total anguish and said something that left me astounded. He said, "Because if you are black they hate you more." He cried so hard that I took him in my arms so that he couldn't see that I too was shedding a tear or two myself. I was hurt for both of my sons, and I was hurt with them.

I was stunned. How could I have let myself be so busy trying to provide for my family, that I didn't realize how I had not equipped them for the harsh realities of a world that can at times be both cold and unwelcoming to those who are outside of our "norm?" Do not misunderstand me, I know all too well from my own experiences, how things can be when you are a minority in a majority world. But what I didn't know was that this 7-year-old had encountered this level of anguish at such an early age, and that he had resolved in his own way that if he could avoid getting any blacker, he might not have to feel the painful consequences of looking different. I doubt that it was overt racism, no sheets draped over the heads of the KKK, or Rodney King style beat downs in the back of the school. No, these were tears running down the face of a child who had been victimized by subtle covert racist distinctions right in front of my face and I didn't even know it was happening in his world.

I sat on the floor holding two weeping children as my wife and I began to explain what a gift it is to be yourself, and to love who you are and how you are made. I told them how wonderfully God has created them in the skin they were in! It led to one of the richest, most rewarding discussions of my children's lives and they still refer to it to this day!

It was then that it became crystal clear, the importance of teaching our children the value of being African American and the value of their own self-worth. Sadly when one speaks of this teaching – African Americans to love themselves, their community or accomplishments, many outside of the realities of our life relegate such pride inappropriately as prejudice. I dare say that no race is exempt from prejudice and blacks, like all people, can have their biases. But pride and prejudice are not the same thing at all. In fact, without the conscious effort to give black children the supplement of self esteem to replace the steady diet sent through media and other methods of communication that subtly suggest inferences of inferiority, they live with a disadvantage that is difficult to overcome in early ages. Our children desperately need to see people who look like them, who have done well and have been accepted by mainstream America so they will know that it is possible.

Today we are seeing more black, brown, and female faces slipping through the glass ceiling to positions of prominence and finding there a new breed of more accepting people. We all need a conscious concerted effort to help showcase these persons to whom young Blacks, Latinos and girls can aspire. Still, we who are in the village that cares for children of all races must be careful to ensure we do not innocently or consciously malign innocent minds with insensitivity to the unique nuances of their needs.

Looking back at that moment with my sons, my regret at that moment was that I had not started sooner. My tears resulted from outrage and shame. I was outraged because the children who I loved were dealing with such hideous experiences so early; and I was ashamed that I was so busy struggling to feed them that I did not think to equip them sooner for the harsh realities to which I naively thought they had not experienced. I was wrong!

This lack of "self-love" and the negative self-image that accompanies it is not limited to those children raised in the inner city. Though my wife and I were struggling financially at the time, my older children were never raised in the inner city and grew up in what would be ordinary neighborhoods of moderate- to middle-class income. No sagging pants, no boom boxes, and no gangs were prevalent at the time. Instead they attended what I thought were good schools. We had low crime, well manicured lawns, active PTA and youth programs – the true American dream. Believe it or not, it is easy to become almost invisible in even these otherwise wholesome environments. Their classrooms were predominantly white, the teachers, principals and staff were generally white, their sports and cheerleading teams were primarily white, as were the dances and birthday parties they attended. Without a strong injection of self-worth and appreciation for their differences, these types of experiences can leave many children of color losing themselves, trying to fit in with others.

If one takes a look at many of the social ills that haunt the African-American community – the proliferation of gangs, teenage pregnancy, illiteracy, high school drop out rates, lower test scores – much of it can be tied back into a lack of self appreciation of who they are. To be sure, many of our families have been self-destructive, and some have been admittedly extremely dysfunctional.

There is no question that we are not without some blame for many of the challenges we face today. The self-esteem issues are exasperated by absentee fathers, substance abuse, and many other circumstances that add to the conundrum of the lagging behind of our people. Yet, I shared my story to say that even when a black family overcomes those hurdles, the father is at home, the family is stable, and the parents are involved with the school, etc., there is still an added invisible weight that saddles down the mind and cripples the soul of our children at incredibly early ages.

The baggage of being different is only crippling when the child is left to carry it without an intentional awareness of cultural diversity, sensitivity training and supervision in private and public schools to ensure that what they learn at school is education and not the devaluation that comes when those who make decisions do not look like the ones they decide about.

I am reminded of the young mainstream girls that we have seen and read about because of their struggle with bulimia and anorexia. They are bombarded with images everywhere you turn of rail thin women and are told, this is beautiful. Similarly, my children were bombarded with images of blonde, straight hair, blue-eyed children and were told this is beautiful. Their perception of normal was skewed based on their surroundings. The take away message is that if you are going to integrate the class, the staff, the pictures, the books, then all involved must reflect that commitment to ensure a healthy environment for those we seek to serve.

If all else fails, it must be the responsibility of the parents to instill the worth and value into our children as early and as often as possible. We must not shirk that responsibility. But if we can gain help from all people to make sure that no person is left dreading the skin they are in, we will really be the people that God meant for us to be. If people in general, and children in particular, are not exposed to their own culture, music, dance and food, all of us have to work to make sure that they experience that exposure. They must see images on the wall and around them that reflect their characteristics, and teach them to enjoy their unique appearance, language, skin tone or whatever it may be that sets them at risk of being a part.

Dr. Martin Luther King Jr.'s words still ring soundly today, "Judge me on the content of my character and not the color of my skin." Can a brother get a good Amen? — Bishop T.D. Jakes

Today's reading in Ezekiel 16:6-14, states clearly how the Lord passed us when we had blood all over us. He cleaned us up, bathed us, applied perfume, dressed us in silk, adorned us in precious jewelry and watched us grow and develop. African Americans have truly come a long way but we have a long way to go. By the grace of God we won't die where we are!

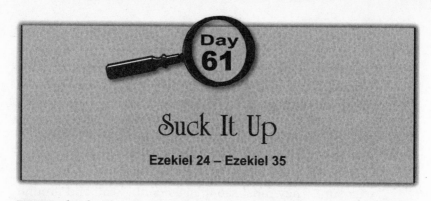

Suck It Up

Ezekiel 24 – Ezekiel 35

Today has been a long day for me. I left Connecticut at 5:30 this morning to ride to New York and then fly to Chicago with a thirty minute layover. I finally arrived in Bloomington, Illinois. I landed here to be met by a delegation of pastors who, as I write, are waiting for me to finish so I can accompany them to the welcome luncheon they have so graciously prepared. I am hungry and want to take a nap. I could also use a long hot shower and I need to get my mind ready for tonight. However, the price of ministry requires you to do a lot of what you do not want to do, or to postpone what you would like to do or even to do what you thought you would never have to do.

In today's reading, I was aghast when my eyes fell upon Ezekiel 24:16 - 24. The Lord told Ezekiel He was about to take away Ezekiel's wife through the vehicle of death in just one moment. Ezekiel was not to weep or cry, nor yell above a whisper. He was to bind on his turban and put on his shoes. Sure enough, that same night his wife was taken away from him and he could not show his grief or distress. God said this is a prototype of what is going to happen to your sanctuary and your nation, but you are not to show the enemy any emotion. Find the strength to persevere, even if on the inside you are falling apart and screaming for your dear life. Further the Lord said, 'Follow what Ezekiel has done and you can make it.'

There have been some days, weeks and even months where I felt like I wanted to cry, fall apart and lay out, but God's grace has kept me together. I am sure many of you have been at that exact same juncture. Something went awry on the job, startling news on the phone, shocking letter in the mail, bad report from the

114

doctor, outrageous bill out of nowhere. You have no idea how you have kept it together. The apostle Paul said, "Your strength is made perfect in weakness." Marvin Sapp sang recently, "I never would have made it but I'm STRONGER and I'm wiser."

One of my favorite lines from the movie *The Great Debaters* is, "Do what you gotta do until you can do what you want to do." So, whatever you are dealing with, suck it up! You are stronger than you think.

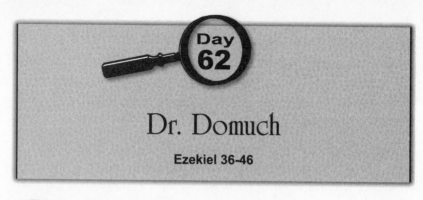

Dr. Domuch

Ezekiel 36-46

One of my eldest daughter Topaz's favorite movies is Eddie Murphy's, *Dr. Dolittle*. She is awed and enthralled at his ability to talk to animals when nobody else can. The greater gift is not the fact he can talk to them, but that he can understand what they are saying as well. After displaying the gift to one, they put the word out and many started banging on his door because they heard of his uncanny ability to hear and heal. All the more encouraging, but of lesser popularity is Dr. Dolittle 2. Towards the end of the movie, it is discovered that the doctor's daughter has the same gift as her father. She can both hear and heal. What a tremendous glow of hope, just to know we have been empowered anointed and equipped to do what the father can. Even Jesus said at the close of the gospels, "Greater things than these will you be able to do." Additionally, every parent should be encouraged to know your children can inherit your gifts and not your weaknesses or curses.

In Ezekiel 39:17, the Lord says "As for you, son of man, speak to the birds of every sort and all beast of the field: assemble and come." Even when we read the favored Sunday school story Noah's ark, he was instructed to gather them but never to talk to them. In the very beginning, Adam was given authority over them, but never told to talk to them! Maybe he should have never talked to the serpent in the first place. Through Ezekiel you see that you can talk to all the animals around you, the dogs that hound you, the chicken heads chasing you, the snakes trying to deceive you, the wolves in sheep clothing and the leeches who want to live off of you. Even David said, *"When the enemy comes to eat up my flesh . . . they will stumble and fall."* Psalm 27:2 He had to be talking about wild animals.

If you are in a zoo-like experience in your life, do not call on Eddie Murphy because he can not do much. If you call on Jesus, He will not do little because He is Dr. Domuch!

116

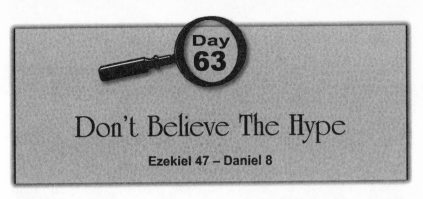

Don't Believe The Hype

Ezekiel 47 – Daniel 8

In the mid-eighties arose a group named Public Enemy, also known as PE. It was a hip-hop group from Long Island, New York, known for its politically charged lyrics, criticism of the media, and active interest in the concerns of the African American community. In 2004, *Rolling Stone Magazine* ranked Public Enemy number forty-four on its list of the *Immortals: 100 Greatest Artists of All Time*. The group was inducted into the Long Island Music Hall of Fame in 2007.

In 1988, they released an album entitled *"It Takes a Nation of Millions to Hold Us Back"* widely regarded as the group's magnum opus. The album regularly ranks as one of the greatest and most influential recordings of all time in various publications. The second single of that album was entitled *"Don't Believe the Hype."* The song's lyrics are mostly about the political issues that were current in the U.S. at the time of its release. In the group was a lyricist and hype man named Flavor Flav. With all of the praise, money and honor from others, he found himself believing the hype of his own success, which in turn led to several run ins with the law. He was arrested numerous times on assault and drug charges and a drug overdose led him into rehab. At this current time, Flavor Flav is acting on reality TV shows which contradict the very lyrics of the songs he wrote in the past, which led to his fame in the beginning.

In today's reading, we have ended the book of Ezekiel and started the book of Daniel. As the book starts, we are introduced to King Nebuchadnezzar II. He reigned as the most powerful king from 605 - 562 B.C. His brilliance as a military leader and his architectural accomplishments are well known even to us today.

King Nebuchadnezzar built one of the Seven Wonders of the Ancient World, the Hanging Gardens of Babylon. He improved canals and restored old religious monuments. He warred with and defeated Egypt, Tyre, Edom, and Judah.

As King Nebuchadnezzar grew in power and might, he started to believe his own hype and grew very prideful (Daniel 4:30). Pride is one of those things God hates (Proverbs 8:13) and God made King Nebuchadnezzar an example. God drove the king from men and made him dwell with the beasts of the field. King Nebuchadnezzar roamed the wild land and was forced to eat grass for seven years. Finally, the king was 'brought to his senses' when he acknowledged God as the King of heaven, "Because everything He does is right and all His ways are just. And those who walk in pride He is able to humble" (Daniel 4:37).

When I read this today my heart began to ache to see how someone so great and powerful could end up losing everything. We may accomplish many things in life, receive great praise and honor from man, but we must remember to stay grounded and focused on the One who has brought it all about. Many times when we start off in things we start off humble and small in our own eyes and depending on God in everything that we do. But after some time, if we are not careful, a dangerous enemy arises called 'pride'. We begin to think our education, money, relationships, status and fame brought us to where we are today. Sometimes we tend to lose sight of God in all that we do. He blesses us with a beautiful home, then we become too busy cutting the lawn and decorating to attend church and give Him praise. He blesses us with a great career and we become too tired to fellowship with Him anymore. He makes our name great among men and we become too important to speak to people. He blesses us with fortune and then we become too frugal to pay our tithes. The reality is all it takes is one-phone call from the doctor, one pink slip from your job, one wrong decision or one 1-night stand to lose it all. Whatever it is God has blessed you with, do not forget to give him the glory no matter what.

Remember to continue to put your trust in God and Him alone. There used to be a saying, "Never forget the bridge that has brought you over because you will need to cross back over it one day." The Bible says, *"Some trust in chariots and others in horses, but we will trust in the name of our God."* (Psalm 20:7) As you go through this day, do not forget to pray, praise, and fellowship with God. "Don't Believe the Hype", because without Him, you are nothing and are destined to fail.

Mercy Me, Mercy Me

Daniel 9 – Hosea 12

One of my absolute favorite R&B artists of all times is Marvin Gaye. (Those of you who just listen to gospel music please pray for me). If I was stranded on a deserted island one of the albums I would have to have with me is his perennial classic, *What's Going On?* Aside from James Brown and Curtis Mayfield, no one else had their finger on the pulse of what was taking place in Black America at the time. Marvin Gaye could have actually done the soundtrack for CNN's special, *Being Black in America.* Growing up in a pastor's house, I think Marvin Gaye's records and the Temptations' Christmas album was the only secular music we had. One of the missing links of today's rap music is that much of it bespeaks the trials, but not much to the triumphs or hope of African American people. Marvin Gaye's song, *Mercy Mercy Me,* is giving a plaintiff cry that what he needs is mercy for all the ill and ails the time have wrought into his life.

Mercy is the twin sister to grace. When a guilty criminal stands before a judge, he or she begs for the mercy of the court for a lenient sentence. When a child is on the brink of failing a class, they may petition the teacher for mercy so they do not have to repeat the class or grade. (I will be a witness!) If someone is late paying a bill and consequences and repercussions are eminent, they can call customer service for mercy in order to get an extension or to negotiate. It is an altogether different set of circumstances, however, when you seek out mercy from God. The first thing you must reconcile in seeking mercy is knowing that you are guilty and that a penalty is due.

The children of Israel became flagrant in their sin and lifestyle and God was fed up with their antics and actions. When we turn to the first chapter of Hosea, it almost reads like a final cut off notice or a pink slip. God uses the prophet's life as a living illustration. He tells him to marry a harlot because that is how God feels about being connected to us who have been unfaithful. To add insult to injury he says in verse six, "You shall have a daughter and you will name her Lo-Ruhamah (No Mercy). Can you imagine having that name on your driver's license, passport or caller ID.? God told Hosea, "Your child will be called 'no mercy' because you will not receive any from me!"

A life without mercy and grace is simply not living. Every day we sin by thought, word and/or deed. The Bible says the wages of sin is death, BUT the gift of God is eternal life! We all should be dead because of our lifestyle and habits, but Jesus granted us mercy on the cross.

As you start another day, before you complain and criticize, think about what you actually deserve from God. *It oughta make you wanna holler and throw up both of your hands and cry Mercy Mercy Me!*

Make A Wish

Hosea 13 – Amos 8

I am amazed, if not horrified, how demonic entities have become sources of entertainment in modern western culture. Take a moment at your leisure to scroll through your cable guide and see how much of the programming centers around satanic scripts. Much of it is aimed at teenagers and preteens in the early afternoon hours when school has been dismissed. The greatest selling children's book of all times is not Mother Goose or Dr. Seuss, but rather *Harry Potter*. Amazingly all of the volumes in the series eclipse 700 pages and kids around the world are reading every page like its crack for a crack head. The storyline is about a young boy training to be a sorcerer and enrolled in a school that teaches him black magic.

When I was growing up our only options were: *I Dream of Jeannie* and *Bewitched*. Whatever the subtleties or nuances, the central characters posed as agents of change, not ambassadors of darkness.

Kids on front stoops or in schoolyards, synagogues and sanctuaries would allow their imaginations to run wild as they played a game called, *Make a Wish*. We all naively believed that if we found a genie in a bottle and rubbed it, we could wish for anything at all and it would come to pass. We could wish to have all the money in the world, be the strongest in the world or the fastest and even pick out whatever kind of car we wanted. Regrettably, none of our wishes ever came true, even when we had the best of intentions.

In the book of Joel, it begins to read as a tragedy in the history of humanity. It foretold locusts are en route to unearth and to devour any and everything with substance. There is a call given for repentance for us to plead for His grace and mercy for all the wickedness we have participated in.

In Chapter 2, the day of the Lord is announced and His wrath and vengeance were about to take full course. In His recourse, nothing or no one would be able to intervene. Thankfully, God's grace and mercy always prevails. Before Chapter 2 end, God exudes pity. In verse 19, He tells them He will send three things people normally would not wish for: grain, wine and oil.

- Grain symbolizes strength. It is necessary to build back up after you come through a major battle and endured some loss.

- Wine symbolizes joy. Sometimes you can go through so much, you lose your joy, laughter, happiness and zeal for living. God wants you to be happy.

- Oil symbolizes the anointing. The anointing destroys the yoke. It positions you for power, covers you in controversy and directs your destiny.

I pray today you do not have to wish for anything; but that you have assurance He is sending you grain, wine and oil

Talking To Phantoms

Amos 9 – Nahum 3

The Spirit of the Lord woke me up early this morning to have time with Him and to read His Word. My spirit was spry, but my body was having difficult trying to obey. I found my thoughts filled with numerous wants that morning. I wanted the sun to stay hidden for one more hour. I wanted the pages of Obadiah, Jonah, Micah and Nahum to read themselves to me, I wanted my clothes to assemble themselves and fall into my suitcase on their own. I wanted my car to go to the gas station and fill up so I would not have to stop on my way to take my girls to school. Realizing my wants were unlikely to occur, I got out of the bed and started listening for God as I began to dutifully, albeit reluctantly, to read today's assignment.

As I inched through the pages of Jonah, it dawned on me God is altogether super bad. He not only talks to people, He also has the ability to talk to things. If you read the book of Jonah with careful scrutiny, you will be amazed at all the actors the Lord brings on to the stage of this narrative. In Chapter 1, Jonah receives a clear call from God and intentionally boards a ship to head in the opposite direction. In verse 4, God hurls a great wind in the direction of the boat Jonah is on. Unlike Jesus, he was not saying, *"peace be still"* but rather sent confusion and strife. Sometimes God will send mayhem into your life just to get your attention.

The text says the crew of the ship worshipped other gods, but in verse 14 they cried out to the one true God. He answered them and said what to do with Jonah. God will even speak to heathens in order to get the purpose of your life fulfilled.

In verse 17, God appointed a great fish to swallow Jonah and then in chapter 2 verse 10, tells the fish to release him. God will speak to your stronghold when it is time for you to be delivered!

In chapter 4 verse 6, God spoke to a plant to cover Jonah from the relentless rays of the sun, and then in verse 7, He has a worm to eat the plant! God spoke to animals, plants, water and sinners to aid Jonah in his growth and development.

Today I hope you know God is not speaking to you alone about your purpose, but also to everything around you. He speaks to disease and tells it to shrink. He speaks to bills and tells them to be patient and wait their turn. He will speak to your supervisor and co-workers to get them off your back or give you a raise. He may tell the gas in your tank to increase so you can complete your assignment for today. He will even speak to your house while your away and command it to be a place of peace and tranquility when you get home.

I pray the Lord tells a Rolls Royce Phantom black on black to make a home in my garage so I can get to the airport with ease (and tells the dealer to keep the note)!

Join "Forbes" List

(Rev Ronnie Nsubuga)
Habakkuk 1— Zechariah 10

Not long ago, I read through the latest Forbes list of the richest people in America. I hoped to find some new names, but there were none. The list does not reflect a dynamic and elastic economy; instead, it reflects a growing concentration of wealth and economic power.

One analysis I made is the richest people trade information. We would not be reading the Bible today if brilliant minds had not taken the time to document their information. Today, information is machines; knowledge is people. Information becomes knowledge when it takes on a social life. Therefore, knowledge lies in databases rather than people.

The existing social and economic gaps are due to the difference in knowledge. The people who seem to have it all together have an endless amount of passion and determination to know more. They always keep coming up with great ideas and are not afraid to act on them.

In our reading today, Habakkuk gives us the tools necessary to be powerful and then some. God speaks to the prophet and the people he represents; *"Write the vision; make it plain so that others may run with it."* (Habakkuk 2:2) No matter how impressive your achievements may be to date, you have the ability to do more than what you have done if you begin to document. Write down what you want, and what you think is required to obtain what you want. In other words, you need a plan. You need to know WHY you are doing WHAT you are doing, as well as HOW you are going to get WHERE you want to be. It is not enough to state you want to make money or that you want to have a business.

You need to write it all down and be specific about the details. There is power in writing down your intentions.

If you want to become one of the wealthiest, you will need to start expanding your perceptions of your capabilities. The least painful way to do this is to start small and work your way up. Get a sheet of paper and write down what you believe yourself to be capable of right now. Think about the dreams you have for your life and the goals you want to work toward. Write them down if you believe they are possible. Write down your ideas for how you might expand your goals. As you continue, expand your faculty by reading more about your field of interest. The more you see for yourself, the more you will be motivated to do something about it. Write it, memorize it and make it personal. In the end, you will be reviewed on the list of the wealthiest.

It's Time To Cross Over!!!!!!

Zechariah 11 – Matthew 4

In today's reading, we 'cross over' from the Old Testament to the New Testament. We leave the old things behind us and run with great speed and joyous anticipation towards the wonderful new things which await us. We have been through the wilderness, faced famines, felt like we were in exile, crossed rivers, run from enemies, and hidden in caves; but in the end we made it.

I pray as you review the journey we have taken; you will begin to thank God for the journey, as well as the progress you have made in your own life. It may have had some hills and valleys, set backs, attacks, disappointments, discouragements, victories and some failures; but in the end you made it. Everyday you live now is a day of new opportunities, choices, dreams, visions, and direction.

As you read today's passages, thank God for bringing you through the old, and then praise him for the new horizon which awaits you because you have now "crossed over."

In Matthew Chapter 2, our Lord and Savior Jesus is born. They shall call His name Emmanuel (God with us) and if He be for us, who can be against us?

The thirty-nine books of the Old Testament are broken up as such:

Pentituch – 5 books

- Genesis - Creation, the fall, the flood, spread of the nations, Abraham, Isaac, Jacob, and Joseph; enslavement in Egypt.

- Exodus - Enslavement, Moses, 10 plagues, Passover, leaving Egypt, Red Sea crossing, Mount Sinai and the 10 Commandments

- Leviticus-Instructions on sacrificial system and the priesthood. Instructions on moral purity.

- Numbers - Still at Mount Sinai, people make false idol and receive punishment. 40 years wandering begins.

- Deuteronomy - Moses' discourses on God's Acts for Israel - the Decalogue, the ceremonial, civil, & social laws, and covenant ratification.

History - 12 books

- Joshua - First half of Joshua describes the seven year conquest of the Land of Promise. The last half deals with partitioning the lands to the people.

- Judges - Time of Judges. This was a bad time period. The Israelites did not drive out all the inhabitants of Canaan and began to take part in their idolatry. Seven cycles of foreign oppression, repentance, and deliverance. In the end, the people failed to learn their lesson.

- Ruth - Kinsman redeemer in Boaz, redeeming Ruth, a Moabitess. Speaks of righteousness, love, and faithfulness to the Lord.

The next 6 books trace the time from Samuel to captivity

- First Samuel - Samuel carries Israel from judges to King Saul

- Second Samuel - David as King, adultery and murder.

- First Kings - Solomon, Israel is powerful. Solomon dies, then division of tribes occurs: 10 to the north and two to the south.

- Second Kings - The Divided Kingdom. All 19 kings of Israel were bad; therefore, captivity in Assyria (722 B.C.). In Judah, eight of twenty rulers were good, but Judah also went into exile.

- First Chronicles - Recounting of the history of Israel to the time of Solomon.

- Second Chronicles - Continued recounting of the life of Solomon and building of temple to captivity. History of Judah only.

The next three books deal with Israel's Restoration.

- Ezra - Cyrus let most of the Jews return to their land of Israel. Zerubbabel led the people (539 B.C.). Ezra returned later with more Jews (458 B.C.). Built the temple.

- Nehemiah - Building the walls of Jerusalem. Nehemiah received permission from the king of Persia to rebuild the walls (444 B.C.). Revival in the land.

- Esther - Took place during chapters 6 and 7 of Ezra. Mordecai. Plot to kill the Jewish people.

Poetry - 5 books

- Job - a righteous man tested by God. Deals with God's sovereignty.

- Psalms - Consists of five divisions which correspond with the five books of the Pentituch. Worship in song. Large variety of subjects

- Proverbs - Practical wisdom for everyday affairs.

- Ecclesiastes - All is vanity. The wisdom of man is futility.

- Song of Solomon - A song between Solomon and his Shulamite bride. Displays the love between a man and a woman.

Prophecy - 17 books

Major Prophets - 5 books

- Isaiah - Looks at the sin of Judah and proclaims God's judgment. Hezekiah. Coming restoration and blessing.

- Jeremiah - Called by God to proclaim the news of judgment to Judah. God establishes a New Covenant.

- Lamentations - Five lamenting poems. Description of defeat and fall of Jerusalem.

- Ezekiel - He ministered to the Jews during their captivity in Babylon. Also includes description of the end of times.

- Daniel - Many visions of the future for the Jews and the Gentiles.

Minor Prophets - 12 books

- Hosea - Story of Hosea and his unfaithful wife, Gomer. Represents God's love and faithfulness and Israel's spiritual adultery. Israel will be judged and restored.

- Joel - Proclaims a terrifying future using the imagery of locusts. Judgment will come, but blessing will follow.

- Amos - He warned Israel of its coming judgment. Israel rejects God's warning.

- Obadiah - A proclamation against Edom, a neighboring nation of Israel, that gloated over Jerusalem's judgments. Prophecy of its utter destruction.

- Jonah - Jonah proclaims a coming judgment upon Nineveh's people. However, they repented and judgment was spared.

- Micah - Description of the complete moral decay in all levels of Israel. God will judge but will also forgive and restore.

- Nahum - Nineveh has gone into apostasy (approx. 125 years after Jonah) and will be destroyed.

- Habakkuk - Near the end of the kingdom of Judah, Habakkuk asks God why He is not dealing with Judah's sins. God says He will use the Babylonians. Habakkuk asks how God can use a nation that is even worse than Judah.

- Zephaniah - The theme is developed of the day of the Lord and His judgment with a coming blessing. Judah will not repent, except for a remnant which will be restored.

- Haggai - The people failed to put God first by building their houses before they finished God's temple; therefore, they had no prosperity.

- Zechariah - Zechariah encourages the Jews to complete the temple. Many messianic prophecies are also included.

- Malachi. - God's people are lax in their duty to God and are growing distant from God. Moral compromise. Proclamation of coming judgment.

Look how far you have come!

Abuse It And You Lose It

Matthew 5 – Matthew 15

Today a congressional representative from Alaska faced charges of corruption. He has been a major voice on Capitol Hill for leadership, finance and military endeavors. In a season where foreclosures are reaching 2.3 million before the close of the year, unemployment has reached 5.7% - the highest its been in four years. In a time where the IRS is projecting bankruptcies to exceed any historical precedent, here is a representative who has influence, contacts and prestige being prosecuted for corruption charges under the umbrella of allegedly taking $250,000 dollars under the table for home improvements. He may very well lose his position, tarnish his party, disgrace his family and maybe even spend time in jail. If he was just a plumber or bus driver, it probably would not be an issue; but he is under greater scrutiny because of his power and the fact his acceptance of the gift is a sign of abusing power.

In Matthew Chapter 10, we eavesdrop on the orientation of Heaven's congressional representatives. They are told to take authority over unclean spirits, cast out demons, and heal every disease and affliction. What awesome power! To abuse that power would be to only heal those they liked, only deal with socially accepted diseases and to only confront the demons they themselves did not wrestle with.

In Matthew Chapter 7, it gives us a glimpse of the teacher's lesson plan by surveying his own life's example. The writer gives us a panoramic perspective of the pupils' position. In verses 28 and 29 it says, ". . . *when Jesus finished these sayings, the crowds were astonished at His teaching for He was teaching them as one who had authority and not as their scribes.*"

What had He just finished teaching? In Chapter 5, He taught on dealing with anger, lust, divorce, retaliation and handling your enemies. In Chapter 6, He taught on giving to the needy, how to pray, and fasting, as well as not having anxiety. In Chapter 7, not judging others, bearing good fruit and building your house right. God has given us authority over everything that would distract us, subtract from us, seduce us and reduce us. We can not abuse that authority by leading others down the wrong path.

A police officer is armed with two articles - a badge and a gun. The badge is his authority and the gun is his power. The badge identifies who he is and the gun enforces it. Your authority is the cross and your gun is the Holy Ghost. Do not abuse the power God has given you. Help somebody and do not hurt anybody.

Gas Up Your Engines!

Matthew 16 – Matthew 26

How many of you have ever run out of gas? In most cases, this would be nearly everyone. AAA reports every year at least a half million people call for help because they have run out of gas. In addition to flat tires, dead batteries, and misplaced keys, running out of gas ranks right up there in the reasons why people call for roadside service. One might understand this happening a generation ago when gas gauges were not entirely accurate and when all the warning lights of our day were non-existent. But now we have warning messages to tell us the fuel is running low (giving us perhaps another hour of driving), and then additional progressively urgent warnings indicating just how many estimated miles of driving we have left. One must say that most people who run out of fuel are "without excuse."

In today's reading, Jesus gives some very profound lessons to His disciples in the form of parables. Amongst them is the parable of the ten virgins. The delay of the bridegroom plays a critical role in the story. Had the bridegroom not delayed, all of the virgins would have been ready and waiting when the marriage procession arrived and they all would have accompanied the bridegroom to the feast.

Because the bridegroom was delayed, half of the virgins were caught unprepared and not able to accompany him to the feast. The wisdom of the wise virgins consisted in their understanding that the bridegroom might be delayed. Why did the wise virgins take the flask of extra oil with them? Was it not because they had the foresight to anticipate they might have to wait? Had they thought there would be no delay, it would have been completely unnecessary for them to carry extra oil. In the end, the only crime of the foolish virgins was not being ready to follow the bridegroom to the feast when finally he came. The bridegroom's response to the crime of these foolish virgins is severe. He bars them from entering the marriage feast altogether; and more severely, he makes the astounding claim that he does not know them.

I know we have all believed God for some great things, but unfortunately it may not have come to pass in the time frame we had expected. Like the five foolish virgins, we become complacent and unprepared; then all of a sudden here it comes, but we are not ready to receive it or walk in it.

In life, the major reason people fail is failing to prepare for the unexpected. It is not enough to just get ready, but we must stay ready. During this week, all I want you to do is to get ready and stay ready for the unexpected because if He promised it, it is destined to come to pass. Your only job is to not run out of gas on this journey called faith due to failure to prepare for the unexpected.

Always remember - a delay is not a denial. The Bible tells us in Habakkuk 2:3 *"For the vision is yet for an appointed time; but at the end it shall speak, and not lie. Though it tarries,, wait for it; because it will surely come, it will not tarry."* So be like the five wise virgins and fill your gas tank because what God has promised will surely come to pass.

The Beginning Of Something Big

Matthew 27 – Mark 8

Yesterday was one of those services that will stay with you for a long time. I was pleased proud and privileged to have my father, Bishop John Richard Bryant, as the guest preacher for both 9:30 and 11:30 (the messages were different and you need to hear both.)

The 9:30 sermon was entitled; *Do You Know Your Value?* He spoke about the treasure that resonates in all of us.

The 11:30 was my personal favorite. It was entitled *How Big are Your Dreams?* In this message, he dealt with the dysfunction that affected the life of Joseph and how his problem was his dreams were too small because they only included himself. That is, until he went through some things like the pit and prison prior to the palace. When he walked out the prison, his dreams enlarged because he now started to interpret the dreams of others. He also began to dream about seeing a way for others. All of us who were in 11:30 service left in a daze, anticipating the opportunity to dream.

I woke up this morning asking myself as I was going through today's reading. "I wonder what Jesus dreamed about?" Of course I do not know, but I imagine it had to be HUGE! Everything Jesus did was for somebody else rather than Himself.

In Mark Chapter 1, Jesus shows His largess and humility by coming to John the Baptist to be baptized. He submitted to somebody less than Himself in order to prepare Himself. Are you willing to do the same?

Immediately after being baptized by immersion, He had to go

through a season of <u>temptation</u>. It seems in the season we are experiencing, everybody wants elevation, but very few can handle temptation.

After Jesus comes through temptation, He begins <u>proclamation</u>. You do not have anything to say on God's behalf until you have come through something. Consequently, you should have a lot to say today!

The next step in His journey is <u>association</u>. Here He picks His first disciples. We really ought not to pick our associates until we know our call and purpose.

The association phase is followed by <u>extermination</u>. Here is where Jesus begins to cast out demonic spirits. You must not be afraid to rid yourself of the things in your life that are not of God. This is critical to your process and God's plan.

Finally, Jesus doles out <u>impartation</u> as He heals people of all kinds of diseases. He does not want to see others in pain or under pressure. What are you going to do this week to ease someone's pain and to lighten someone's pressure?

All of this just in the first chapter of Mark! It finally hit me; Jesus must have been dreaming about ME. - and YOU! What a revelation! That calls for celebration!

How big are your dreams? As we begin another week, I earnestly pray you realize you are at the beginning of something BIG!

It's Difficult But It's Doable

Mark 9 – Luke 1

Whenever God calls you, He never calls you to do something easy. It would have been easy for God to tell Noah to build a canoe, but he called him to do something difficult. It would have been easy for God to tell Daniel to pet the lions, but He asked him to sleep in the den with them. It would have been easy if Jesus asked you not to turn the right cheek if someone strikes you on the left, but He asked you to turn the other.

In the Beatitudes, Jesus says, "Blessed are you when people insult you, persecute you and falsely say all kinds of evil against you because of Me." This is really difficult to do because He never asks you to do the easy stuff. Many of you are frustrated reading because God is calling you to do a difficult thing.

In Mark Chapter 9, we encounter a boy with an unclean spirit which robbed him of speech (Vs 17). Because he could not talk, the evil spirit threw him to the ground. Whenever you cannot speak for yourself, you lower yourself to the ground. In verse 22, his father knew the boy was in a difficult situation and asked Jesus, *"If you can do anything, take pity on us and help us."* The thing this father never knew was God majors in doing the difficult. In verse 23, Jesus responded, *"Everything is possible for him who believes."*

In Verse 28 the disciples are confused and concerned because they could not drive out the demons, yet they thought they were empowered to handle the difficult. Verse 29 tells us Jesus responded by telling them you can do the difficult only through prayer.

I want to say to all of you facing the difficult; today I dare you to pray. I ask God to help me do the difficult in the midst of a recession. I ask God to help me do the difficult in an economy that is souring. I want to do the difficult!

In Mark 10:23, Jesus looked around and said to his disciples, "How difficult it is for the rich to enter the kingdom of God!" He said difficult but not impossible. I have an unusual prayer request; God make it difficult because I want to get in the Kingdom wealthy. I want to have wealth and wisdom.

On Sunday, Bishop John Bryant asked, "How big are your dreams?"

My dreams are so big that I want the wealth to fly the entire church to the Bahamas on Empowerment Airlines for the conference. It sounds difficult, but it is doable.

Presently, I have conference registrants at Westin and Sheraton Hotels in Bahamas. All the money from these hotels goes to people who are not of the Kingdom. I want the body of Christ to own these hotels! It is difficult, but it is doable.

When the president gives a national address, all programming on national networks is canceled. When I go on air at the conference, I want CNN, FOX News, ABC, and NBC, to go off air. While I am not the president, I am a prophet. While it is difficult, it is doable.

On Saturday when we leave the island, I do not want anybody on the island to remain unsaved. It is difficult, but doable.

Today as you read, pray that God will do something difficult, but doable in your life.

I Hit The Jackpot!

Luke 2 – Luke 9

In the midst of a failing economy, every industry is suffering. According to *Christian Today* magazine, offerings in churches have gone down by 35% due to the current gas prices. Few American families went on vacation this summer; many airlines are cutting down on their routes, hotel industries are seeing a tremendous drop, and the Republican Party is up against the road.

One industry that is booming is gambling especially in Atlanta City and Los Vegas. In the midst of crisis, impoverished people are willing to take their chances. People who are poor in mind think they become rich by chance. The chances are that all your dreams will not come true. The chances are that what you plan for your life is not how life looks. The chances are that you will have more struggles than you have triumphs.

To follow Christ, is an absolute chance; the chance of persecution, affliction and sacrifice. The flip side is Jesus always takes a gamble on us, fully knowing we are prone to backslide. He will always take a risk going against what society deems acceptable.

In Luke 8, Jesus takes a risk after calling his disciples by allowing three women to follow. We know their professions of those called to be disciples, but we do not know their problems. In verse 2, Mary Magdalene is the first woman who follows. From her, Jesus cast seven demons. Verse 3 tells of Joanna, a desperate housewife, and Susanna, who had no reportable means of income. These three women were helping to support the disciples from their own means. Though the Bible does not detail their means of income, we know the woman had finances. These three women took care of thirteen men. All twelve of the disciples had jobs of some sort, but they had not saved enough to care for the Master. Instead, those with no jobs found resources to support the ministry.

Today, be prepared for resources to come from somewhere else. Because you are professional does not mean you will prosper; and because you are unemployed does not mean you do not have options. To follow Jesus, you always hit a jackpot because I have never seen *the righteous forsaken nor their seed begging for bread* (Psalm 37:25). You will hit a jackpot because: He gives seed to the sower and He will give back to you a good measure, pressed down and running over in return for what you give Him. How can it be that three women took care of thirteen men? I am glad you asked. It is because no matter how many people live in your house, you need only three. You do not need Mary, Joanna and Susanna; instead you need the Father, the Son and the Holy Spirit. The moment you get these, you have hit the jackpot.

I Got The Hook Up;
Holla If You Hear Me!

Luke 10 – Luke 19

There is power in the number 2. Two is the first number by which we can divide another. The first time the word two is used in the Bible is in relation to this theme of division. The sun and the moon were to mark out the division between the day and the night. The Son has two natures, human and divine. There are two Testaments, the Old and New. Man is male and female. There are two types of people - sheep and goats. There are two ages - this age and the age to come.

God gives us examples of the power of '2' when He gives Noah the directions of bringing in two animals of every kind of species. He is not saying two of every kind of sexuality. It was not two male goats but rather a male and a female. The reason for this was to foster procreation.

In Luke 10:1, the Lord appointed 72 others and sent them two by two ahead of Him to every town and place where He was about to go. This is exactly the same model we find in Noah's ark. I do not believe these 72 were all male. They had to procreate when they got to town. You cannot just consider the 72; He talks about the 72 and the 12. These 72 others were added to the 12. Therefore Jesus had a staff of 84 disciples. Verse 2, *the harvest is plentiful, but the workers are few.*

I wish in our church we had 84 committed workers, 84 intercessors, 84 liturgical dancers, 84 ministers on staff, 84 parents volunteering for the youth department, 84 on security; but the harvest is so plenteous that even if I had the 84, they still would not be enough.

143

Jesus told them to go 2 by 2 and in verse 3, He says, *"I am sending you out like lambs among wolves."* The reason is because one would act as a distraction and the other a protector. The wolf has limited eye sight; it can only look at one lamb at a time. While the wolf looks at one, the other is covering. Our responsibility is to look out for one another. Verse 4, *"Do not take a purse or bag or sandal."* So now Christ has a staff of 84 and none is getting pain. They are just glad to be in service.

What would happen if any two of you would work for the ministry full time for free (verse 7) and still believe you would eat everyday, believe that your family would be taken care of and also believe that there would be a roof over your head? The problem is we live in an age were people are not committed to any particular church. They seem to disagree with the pastor or do not like the choir, so they move to another church. However, they still need the other to keep them accountable, stable and consistent.

Verse 9 - heal the sick. In other words, one is to lay hands and the other is to catch whoever falls.

Verse 13 speaks of the miracles in you and not the miracles around you. According to verse 13, in order to see miracles, you ought to first feel the miracle. Today expect God to do a miracle in you, for you to move from anger to being pleasant, from being depressed to having joy, from sickness to health. I do not know who of you is reading this, but two of you are going to have a miracle happen in you.

In verse 17, the 72 returned with joy and said, *'Lord even the demons submit to us in your name.'* That means everybody came back. I believe by faith, if all of you connect with the right person, you will be in service to meet me on Sunday morning. You will come with joy and I am looking forward to it.

While I am in Bahamas, even before I return to Baltimore, I am looking to you to cast out demons in the name of Jesus. Your quest today is to find one more person to travel with, to encourage you, to pray with you and to support you. When you get the hook up; holla if you hear me!

144

It's No Longer Necessary

Luke 20 – John 5

I was at breakfast this morning in the Bahamas with a group of people who are here for our second annual conference. As we went around the table placing our orders, one member requested only pancakes because she no longer eats meat. The entire table was astonished. We told her they have turkey bacon, beef sausage, and pork loin to choose from. She responded, "I don't eat meat anymore." She gave up meat for Lent and it was the hardest 40 days she has ever encountered. She shared that during Lent, she had cravings, thoughts and desires for meat. After she completed the 40 days, she realized it was no longer necessary. She made a commitment for 40 days but after she realized she had lived without it, she has not gone back.

In Luke 22:35, God gives an unusual assignment to the servants - not to take with them any money bags, hand bags or sandals. All these are things that are necessary. I am in the Bahamas, but I can not imagine coming here with no money, no bags to carry my belongings, and no sandals. Every day averages to be about 105 degrees. I cannot imagine walking on the hot sand without sandals or shoes on.

Jesus is saying everything you think you needed for the trip is no longer necessary because it is no longer a trip, but a journey. In this journey, I am now directing you more. It does not require finance, it requires faith. When you are on a journey, God does not want you to cover your feet because the Bible says *"Beautiful are the feet of those that carry the gospel."* (Romans 10:15) This means you will have to step on scorpions and not be bitten.

Can you imagine going away on a journey to a destination you do not know, with no clue on how long you are going to stay? You are trusting God with no money, no bags, and nothing on your feet? That is the prescription of every person who has a call on their lives. You will never have enough money for what God has called you to do. Your journey is leading you to your future so you cannot carry stuff from your past. Many of you are already in the middle of a journey now. In verse 36, Jesus tells them, *"But now if you have a purse, take it, also a bag."* The only thing He does not tell them to bring is sandals. In verse 35, He asked them to leave their money, bags and shoes. But in verse 36, He asks them to leave their shoes because there will always be a part of you that will be exposed, a part of you that will always be vulnerable. Then He says, *"If you don't have a sword, sell your cloak and buy one."* So now I have no shoes and no cloak, but I have a sword because I have to fight over issues of finance and issues of my past.

In verse 38, one of the disciples says, *"Lord, look, here are two swords."* What this says is that you have the money, but the stuff you were to use your money for, someone will provide. I am living for the day when money will not be necessary. I am living for the day when I do not have to carry anything, whether my degrees, contacts, lineage, or affiliation; but the only thing I have to take with me is the name of Jesus.

Facing Your Family

John 6:1 – John 15:17

This morning we honor the life and legacy of Bernie Mac, one of the most controversial and outspoken comedians of our age. Beyond his language, you must appreciate his creative genius and commitment to family. All of us at one point or another watch the Bernie Mac show depicting the travails in the black family. He adopted his niece and nephews, born by his sister who is battling with drug abuse. On the show he had no children of his own, but treated his sister's as his own and that is family.

Many of you who are reading this may be going through something with your own family right now. As much as they have lied on you, hated you, upset you, criticized you, and judged you, they are still your family. In the book of Genesis, Joseph had the same problem. He had tremendous dreams but he was thrown down by his family. In spite of how they treated him, when Joseph rose to power, he still came back and rescued his family in the midst of famine.

In John Chapter 7, we get a rare look into the family of Jesus. He had at least six siblings. In verses 3 and 4, his brothers said to him, *"You ought to leave here and go to Judea, so that your disciples may see the miracles You do. No one who wants to become a public figure acts in secret. Since You are doing these things, show Yourself to the world."* Then we see a harrowing verse. In all my years of preaching, I have never paid attention to this. In verse 5, even his own brothers did not believe in him. Jesus felt that 12 focused men left their families to follow him and not even his brothers believed him.

Imagine - 5000 people followed Him, but his own brothers did not believed in Him. A woman with an issue of blood for twelve years could touch Him and be healed, but his brothers did not believe Him. Two blind men screamed to get His attention, but his brothers did not believe Him.

Jesus responded, *"You go to the feast. I am not yet going up to this feast, because for Me the right time has not yet come."*

In verse 10, after His brothers left for the feast, He went also; but in secret, not publicly.

On this very day God is going to bless your family in private. Privately intercede for your family, privately pray for your family. Anybody who wants to get the attention of God ought not to do it publicly but privately. The same God who hears in private can bless you publicly.

I will never forget when my mother took me to the store with my sister. She would privately say, "Don't embarrass me when we get in public."

Today, privately call your family member you have not spoken to in a long time. The same way you face your family in the private is how God will bless you in the public.

Power 4 Life!!!!!

John 15 – Acts 5

To read the Los Angeles newspapers in 1906, one might have wondered about all the excitement in an old building on Azusa Street, located in the industrial part of the city. According to the *Los Angeles Times*, a bizarre new religious sect had started with people "breathing strange utterances and mouthing a creed which it would seem no sane mortal could understand." Furthermore, "Devotees of the weird doctrine practice the most fanatical rites, preach the wildest theories, and work themselves into a state of mad excitement." If that didn't grab the reader's attention, the article continued by saying that, "Colored people and a sprinkling of whites compose the congregation, and night is made hideous in the neighborhood by the howling of the worshippers who spend hours swaying forth and back in a nerve-racking attitude of prayer and supplication. To top it all off, they claimed to have received the baptism of the Holy Spirit with the evidence of speaking in tongues."

After the gift of salvation through Jesus Christ, of all the other gifts given to mankind by God, there is none greater than the presence of the Holy Spirit. In today's reading Jesus is about to ascend unto heaven to take His seat at the right hand of the Father. He assures His disciples not to be dismayed or discouraged because even though He must go, He is not leaving them alone, but sending them a Helper and Comforter, the Holy Spirit. In the book of Acts on the day of Pentecost, His promise was fulfilled.

The Holy Spirit has many functions, roles, and activities. First, He does a work in the hearts of all people everywhere. Jesus told the disciples that He would send the Spirit into the world to "convict the world of sin, and of righteousness, and of judgment .

. ." (John 16:7-11). Everyone has a "God consciousness" whether they admit it or not, because the Spirit applies the truths of God to men's own minds as to convince them by fair and sufficient arguments that they are sinners. Responding to that conviction brings men to salvation. Jesus said He would send the Spirit to us to be our Helper, Comforter, and Guide. (John 14:16). The Greek word translated here "Helper" means *one who is called alongside and has the idea of someone who encourages and exhorts.* Abiding has to do with His permanent residence in the hearts of believers (Romans 8:9; 1 Corinthians 6:19-20, 12:13). Jesus gave the Spirit as a "compensation" for His absence, to perform the functions toward us, which He would have done if He had remained personally with us. Among those functions is that of revealer of truth. The Spirit's presence within us enables us to understand and interpret the Word. Jesus told His disciples "when He, the Spirit of Truth, has come, He will guide you into all truth . . ." (John 16:13). He reveals to our minds the whole counsel of God as it relates to worship, doctrine, and Christian living. He is the ultimate guide, going before, leading the way, removing obstructions, opening the understanding, and making all things plain and clear. He leads in the way we should go in all things. Without such a guide, we would be apt to fall into error.

Another of His roles is that of gift-giver. First Corinthians 12 describes the spiritual gifts given to believers in order that we may function as the body of Christ on earth. The Spirit gives all these gifts, both great and small, so we may be His ambassadors to the world, showing forth His grace and glorifying Him. The Spirit also functions as fruit-producer in our lives. (Galatians 5:22-23).

Today I want you to take heart because just as Jesus promised the disciples the Comforter, He has made that same promise to you. No matter what it is you may be going through, know that you are not alone. The Holy Spirit, the Comforter, is right there with you every step of the way. He is the gentle Spirit of God that wipes away every one of your tears. He is the peaceful One that quiets all of your storms, and He is the one that prays the will of God for your life when you do not know what you should pray for. He is the One that leads and guides you so you will not lose your way. My prayer for you during this week is that God would refill you with His Holy Spirit. The Bible says there is "one baptism but many refills". I also pray you would walk in the fullness of the power of His Spirit in every area of your lives - in your homes, jobs, churches, communities, wherever you go and whatever you do. God did not send His Spirit for us to just jump, shout and run, but He sent Him for us to have Power 4 Life.

Sleep On It!

Acts 6 – Acts 16

In Genesis, the Lord calls Adam to go to sleep. You need to go to sleep because there are some things God will not do while you are awake. When you are awake, you will need to control, manipulate and manage stuff. Adam had no idea that while he was asleep God was working. He woke up to a new reality, to see something he had never seen before.

Eve is always the beginning of something. It is from Eve that you get Christmas Eve. The anticipation of Christmas does not start until the eve. The most anticipated time in our church is always the New Year's eve because we know we are getting ready to go into something. So Adam awoke on the Eve. I am sure every time he went to sleep after that, he was waking up looking for Eve.

When you turn to our reading today in Acts 7, Stephen is going through a rough day. Verse 54 tells us the reason of all this is because the enemy is grinding his teeth at him. Sometimes the enemy is so angry at you that he will not even speak to you, but grind his teeth instead. So, you should be glad for the people who say they are not speaking to you.

In verses 56 – 57, *"'I see the heaven open and the Son of Man standing at the right had of God!' At this, they covered their ears and, yelling at the top of their voices, they all rushed at him..."*

The enemy can try to ignore you and act like he does not hear you, but he hears your destiny coming and sees your future around the corner. Verse 58 says, *"they dragged him out of the city and began to stone him."* And just like what Jesus did on the cross, in vs. 59, Stephen turned his spirit over to the Master. Sometimes when you feel like you are between the rock and a hard place like

Stephen, turn your spirit over to the Master. Every bill you feel you cannot pay, turn it over to the Master. When your child is out of control, turn him/her over to the Master. When your marriage is in trouble, when your ministry is not growing, turn it over to the master. Verse 60, *"Then he fell on his knees and cried out with a loud voice, 'Father forgive them'."* (Jesus' first words are Stephen's last words) When you turn it over to God, God will turn the order around. The first shall be last and the last shall be first. I am the head and not the tail.

Vs 60b, *"When he had said this, he fell asleep."* The interesting thing is, we never see him wake up. But when he did wake up, he realized it was the best sleep in his life.

This is the first time in 78 days I have ever given you this admonishment - if you can find some time today, take a nap. God is going to set you up for great things. Sleep on it!

What's On Your Altar?

Acts 17 – Acts 27

When commenting about the Olympics, one late night television host said, "*I hope the U.S. team wins enough gold that we can bring it back home and revive the economy that has been lost to China.*"

In every fabric of our community, people are being hit by the reality of this plummeting economy. People are being required to make vital and critical decisions. Splurging is not a question and economizing is the call for the day. In a combination between having minimal options or being slaves to consumerism, many have begun to live off credit cards, thus creating a cycle of debt that may turn out to be disastrous for those who launch out into the deep, buying what they do not need with money they do not have, to impress folk they do not like.

This generation is going to have regrettably the greatest debt ratio in the history of our nation. Of all the industries that are suffering, two surely are not; the petroleum industry and the credit card industry. It is almost as if the populace has come to a consensus we must drive and we must buy without seeing the effect of either. We are not seeing what the smog is doing to the ozone layer or what the hidden fees are doing to your bank account. The average credit card interest rate is charging you between 17-20%. So, whatever you think you have purchased on sale, you have lost the discount to credit card fees.

There is a commercial that has captivated the imagination of millions. In it medieval warriors representing credit card interest are charging towards an unsuspecting consumer. Just before they pounce on him, he pulls out the card of choice which is able to beat back the attack of escalating interest rates. The commercial ends with the catch phrase, "What's in your wallet?" suggesting if you do not have this card, you have the wrong one.

When we read Acts Chapter 17, we find Paul immersed in a community that is in much confusion because they are not sure what they believe. The atmosphere is congested because there were so many doctrines and ideologies, people were believing just about any and everything. When he arrives in Athens, Paul finds the church has not spoken out at all about what is going on in the community.

The American church is going to have to answer the same thing; why have we remained silent in the face of corruption, capitalism, chauvinism and complacency? The bitter pill is, much of it has slipped from outside the church into our pews and pulpits! They reviled and ridiculed Paul because he spoke of the resurrection and it was a theology they had not been introduced to before. In verse 23, Paul states, "... for as I was passing through and considering the objects of your worship, I even found an altar with this inscription: 'TO THE UNKNOWN GOD'.

(WARNING: whenever you introduce a new idea, concept or approach, get ready for controversy, attack and cynicism)

Today, I want to ask you not what is in your wallet but what is on you altar? Some of your worship practices are foreign to the God that we serve. If you feel your situation is going to kill you, what god are you serving? Jesus is known for getting up from the dead. If you think you will be seized by debt and recession, what god are you serving? Ours is known to supply all needs according to His riches in glory! In verse 28 it says, "for in Him we live and move and have our being . . ." The Bible says, "greater is He that's in you than he that's in the world." (I John 4:4)

If you do not know what is in you, then you do not know what you have. What is in your heart should be on your altar (and if you cannot figure it out, here is a hint—He was on the cross). The same God who was on the cross can put something in your wallet!

Something Has Got To Come Out Of This!

Acts 28 – Romans 14

There is a universal law of cause and effect that all of us rest under in the earth. Every action is going to produce a reaction. Seemingly, the children of God act oblivious to this rule. Bishop Rudolph McKissick shared while preaching in the Bahamas last week that we want the presents from God, but we shun the process. As you go through your day, just about everything you touch and encounter requires a process that no doubt has to be painful. The orange juice you drank this morning came out of oranges being crushed. The coffee from Starbucks began as coffee beans that were ground and subjected to intense heat. The diamonds you wear began as coal under immense pressure in order to get its shine on. I dare not even go into what you are going to eat today at the risk of many of you becoming instant vegetarians!

In Romans Chapter 5, Paul attempts to hold our hands at the doctor's office, knowing that the needle is coming from behind the doctor's back. But if we remain steady for the shot, we will not go into shock! The things he expounds in relationship to the process and promise of cause and effect are not popular in the western world's church culture. We want the gain without the pain, a resurrection without a crucifixion. In verse 3 he says, ". . . *rejoice in your suffering . . .*" Quite a difficult task if you ask me. Nonetheless when you are suffering as many of us are today, it is not just about the bill, the health concern, the family matter, the oppressive job. Rejoice in it knowing something is coming out of it you. You are not suffering for nothing! You are rejoicing because your suffering is teaching you endurance. You are stronger now because of things you have been through. You now have a greater tolerance for pain and problems than you did previously. Things which would have crippled you before no longer have the same impact because you now know how to endure.

In verse 4 of Chapter 5, Paul gives us the insight that the process is far from over in that one step. Endurance is going to turn into something else—character. Your reputation is what people think of you in public, your character is who you are in private. God is not interested in our reputation, but in our character. What impresses people matters not to the Master. Who are you when nobody is looking? What would you do and what decisions will you make if you know you will not get caught? What kind of Christian are you behind closed doors? Once you have character, it produces hope. That then says to us you can not have hope if you have no character.

Barack Obama is an awesome prototype of the audacity of hope. His character is impeccable, which makes him globally acceptable. He already won the candidacy of character. After the breaking news with John Edwards last week, its all the more glaring to know the only issue the media and the Republicans could find on Barack Obama was statements by his former pastor! For a black man in his forties, that is huge!

Verse 5 is an insurance policy that says the process is worth it all. Your hope will not allow you to be put to shame. You will not be embarrassed, humiliated or lose faith; not because of your perfection, but because of your hope.

Today as you are reading this and you feel as if you are going through something terribly difficult, pause and ask your self: "What am I getting out of this?" Jesus went through something similar while on the cross. All that pain He endured was to perfect the process of grace, to know that while we were yet sinners, Christ died for us.

As you approach the last days of reading through the Bible, I pray that your early morning and late night readings were not in vain. I pray in earnest that like me, you are getting a lot out of this!

It's Gonna Hurt!!!

Romans 15 – 1 Corinthians 14

Last night I was preaching in Tampa, Florida. My armor bearer was walking very slowly due to excruciating pain. He experienced a toe injury while we were in the Bahamas and his doctor told him to wear soft bottom shoes. Unfortunately, he did not have a pair of soft bottom dress shoes for service last night, so he decided to wear his hard bottom dress shoes. He chose fashion over comfort. This in turn had him walking less than two miles an hour and limping. Unfortunately, he was in no position at all to help me with my needs. This would have never happened if he would have had on the right shoes. The doctor did not tell him the soft bottom shoes would totally alleviate his pain , but he did say they would minimize it.

This morning many of you are faced with what pair of shoes to wear—the soft bottom shoes made for comfort and safety (the Pain of Discipline) or the hard bottom shoes made for fashion only (the Pain of Regret). No matter which pair you decide to wear, they both are going to hurt. The difference is, one will last longer and the other one will be better for you in the long run!

In today's reading, we finished the book of Romans and entered the first book of Corinthians. The Apostle Paul started the church in Corinth. A few years after leaving the church, Paul heard some disturbing reports about the Corinthians church (CHURCH DRAMA). The church was full of pride, the church was excusing sexual immorality, spiritual gifts were being used improperly, and there was rampant misunderstanding of key Christian doctrines. He wrote 1 Corinthians in an attempt to restore the Corinthian church to its foundation – Jesus Christ.

The Corinthian church was plagued by divisions. The believers in Corinth were dividing into groups loyal to certain spiritual leaders (1 Corinthians 1:12; 3:1-6). Paul exhorted them to be united because of devotion to Christ (1 Corinthians 3:21-23). The Corinthian believers were essentially approving of an immoral relationship (1 Corinthians 5:1-2). Paul commanded them to expel the wicked man from the church (1 Corinthians 5:13). The Corinthian believers were taking each other to court (1 Corinthians 6:1-2). Paul taught them it would be better to be taken advantage of than to damage their Christian testimony (1 Corinthians 6:3-8). Paul gave the Corinthian church instructions on marriage and celibacy (1 Corinthians Chapter 7), food sacrificed to idols (1 Corinthians Chapters 8 and 10), Christian freedom (1 Corinthians Chapter 9), the veiling of women (1 Corinthians 11:1-16), the Lord's Supper (1 Corinthians 11:17-34), and spiritual gifts (1 Corinthians Chapters 12-14). He urged them to grow up it the things of God and not to give up, but to discipline themselves and to forget about the pain that comes with following the teachings of Christ, because a greater Hope awaited them.

Today I want you to take a moment and think about the sum total of everything you are currently doing to improve your life, family, relationship with God or business. Think of every detail you can, the level of effort, the sweat, the time—everything. Now think about if you do not do it. Think about the lives that will never be touched and changed, the dreams that will never be accomplished, the businesses that will never get started, and the company that will never have a Christian CEO. Think about the magazine covers that your photo will be missing from and most of all think about the regret you will feel.

Today whether you decide to continue on the road to accomplish the destiny God has for your life, or whether you decide to throw up your hands and walk away, remember this; no matter what you decide, "IT'S GONNA HURT!" However, the pain of discipline weighs mere ounces and will last for a short time, compared to the pain of regret, which weighs tons and can last forever!

It's Coming!

1 Corinthians 15 – Galatians 3

The whole world this morning is tuned into the Olympics, waiting to see if Michael Phelps is going to break and make history by acquiring an astounding eight gold medals. Athletic enthusiast from every field are awaiting to see if in their life time they will be witnessing what many journalist believe is the greatest athlete to live in the 21st century.

In 1972 during the Muich games, Mark Spitz won seven gold medals and set the stage and the standard by which Michael Phelps is being judged. Interestingly enough, when Mark Spitz broke the record, Michael Phelps had not yet been born. On the cover of this morning's USA TODAY, Vicki Michaels stated she does not believe what Michael Phelps is going to accomplish will be topped anytime soon. She argues passionately the keys to his success are many; including his form, the structure by which he approaches the sport, his height (he stands 6'5") and his diversity. Most swimmers are good in one area, such as relay or 100 meters, but Mike dominates in all. What is all the more awe inspiring is the fact he not only wins, but every time he competes, he breaks his own record! Seeing him win his 6th gold medal last night, we all sit on the bleachers of our bedrooms expecting that . . . it's coming!

The book of Galatians is an intriguing treatise of theology; it is light on narrative, but heavy on proposition. In Chapter 2, it argues and articulates our being justified by faith; assessing we ought to all be dead, but for the grace of God and the sacrifice of Christ we are all yet still here.

In Chapter 3, Paul helps us understand where we are as recipients of Grace is not because of the law since we all have broken the law(of the Old Testament). It is also not by works because the work we do for the Kingdom still does not qualify us for the gift of God's grace. Instead, it is because of our faith. Our power to believe in Him is the most powerful tool and weapon we have at our disposal and it is grossly under used.

In verse 22, the dissertation on faith begins to intensify when it states, "*The scripture imprisoned everything under since that the promise of faith in Jesus Christ might be given to those who believe.*" Rejoice in knowing your sin has been sent to prison without parole because you have been reading through the Bible over these 90 days.

In verse 23, it says, "*Before faith came, we were held captive under the law, imprisoned until the coming faith was revealed.*" For those who have been feeling bogged and stifled by circumstances and situations, hold on; your new faith is coming! When the faith you have been stretching for, reading for, praying about and travailing through arrives, the bonds will be broken!

In verse 25, the last verse we are to read for today, it makes a declaration that all of us need to read and remember, *your new faith is here!* All this time you have been hearing in church about it coming, wait on it. The word for today is that it is here! Just before it arrives in verse 24, it states our guardian, Jesus, came that we might be justified.

Take delight in knowing you are anointed to be like Michael Phelps. This year you are going to break all your old records - pray more, study more, have more discipline. You have to get to eight medals because eight is the number of new beginnings and its time for you to have a fresh start. The structure and form of your life is getting ready to change. You are history in the making. Tell the atmosphere, "It's coming!"...Keep in mind whatever feats you accomplish, it is because of a sacrifice made before you were born. No, it is not Mark Spitz. Because of Jesus Christ, get ready to get the gold this weekend. Do not doubt , because by faith - IT'S COMING!

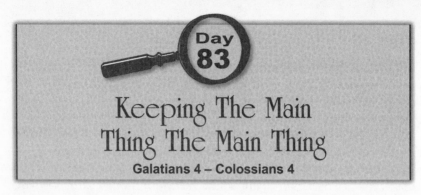

Keeping The Main Thing The Main Thing

Galatians 4 – Colossians 4

I am headed to the airport in Durham, North Carolina after preaching in Kinston, North Carolina last night. On Thursday I was in Mansfield, Ohio, an hour outside Columbus, preaching for one of my sons in the ministry to offer him support in the community to which he has been assigned.

On Wednesday, I was in Tampa, Florida, preaching for the Family Feast conference sponsored by the Church of God. Tuesday, due to some demanding business meetings in Washington, DC, I was not able to make it back for Bible study.

This morning I awoke with a tremendous heaviness of heart; not out of fatigue or weariness, but about the welfare of those whom I have been assigned to pastor. In the age in which we live, multi tasking has become the norm for our times. People are continuously on the phone or working on computers, while watching television, cooking and attending to their families. Amidst all of that, you have to be intentional to keep the main thing the main thing.

The Lord has blessed me to have the capacity to do many things - operate as the head of a family, evangelize, lecture, business, write books, mentor, preach, cast vision and administrate; but above all, I am clear that the main call on my life is to pastor. It matters not what arenas, halls, stadiums or convention centers I am blessed to preach in, there is no greater desire than seeing the people I have been entrusted to pastor at 4217 Primrose— Empowerment Temple.

I hope today you will take a moment and assess, as well as prioritize, what is the main thing you are supposed to be doing in this season of your life. I am confident you are gifted in many areas, but what is your main thing? Our staff is one of the most gifted on the planet, but the beauty of them all is they all know the main thing: Jesus, could heal the sick, raise the dead, feed the multitude, walk on water, teach from sun up to sundown, restore sight to the blind and make the lame walk; however He was clear that the main thing He was set on this earth to do was to die on the cross. Your main thing may be killing you, but if it is what you were born to do, you will rise again.

In our reading today in Ephesians, Paul exposes his true heart. He is a mentor, a bishop, a writer, a motivator and a theologian; but first in his heart, he is a pastor. Listen to his prayer in Ephesians 3:14-20. What he prayed for the church at Ephesus is the same thing I pray for all of you.

14 When I think of all this, I fall to my knees and pray to the Father,

15 the Creator of everything in heaven and on earth,

16 I pray that from His glorious, unlimited resources, He will empower you with inner strength through His Spirit,

17 Then Christ will make His home in your hearts as you trust in Him; your roots will grow down into God's love and keep you strong,

18 and may you have the power to understand, as all God's people should, how wide, how long, how high, and how deep His love is -

19 May you experience the love of Christ, though it is too great to understand fully. Then you will be made complete with all the fullness of life and power that comes from God.

20 Now all glory to God, who is able, through His mighty power at work within us, to accomplish infinitely more than we might ask or think.

New Living Translation

I asked one of my staff members this week to take on an additional assignment and they graciously and respectfully declined saying, "Pastor I've got to keep the main thing the main thing."

Even at the risk of turning something down next week, keep the main thing The Main Thing.

People Do Change

1 Thessalonians 1 – Philemon

On a memorable September night in 1985 at Cincinnati's Riverfront Stadium, Pete Rose transformed his baseball career into something legendary. With hit number 4,192, Rose passed Ty Cobb to become baseball's career leader in hits. At the time, Rose played so hard he was nicknamed Charlie Hustle and was a cinch to be elected to the baseball Hall of Fame. But four years later, Rose was banned from the sport after an investigation discovered he gambled thousands of dollars on baseball games as a player and a manager for the Cincinnati Reds. Rose said he "made some mistakes" but denied betting on baseball.

In 2002 during the World Series game, the commissioner introduced Pete Rose back to the baseball fans. All that could be heard in the stadium was a loud, long ovation and the public chanting, "Hall Of Fame! Hall of Fame!" With their applause and their chant, those fans were stating that they had forgiven Pete Rose for his betting behavior as the Cincinnati Reds' manager. And more important, they were telling the Major League Baseball commission to take him back because he had learned his lesson and "People Do Change."

Today we are reading the books of Thessalonians and Philemon. Philemon is a little book with a big lesson. Paul teaches Philemon about forgiveness, the foundation of Christianity. He wrote this letter to Philemon asking him to forgive his slave, Onesimus, for running away. Philemon was probably a wealthy member of the Church at Colosse. This epistle was not a public document for the Colossians, but a personal letter to Philemon. It was to be shared with Philemon's home church, a small group of believers who met in his home, as it is also addressed to people other than Philemon.

Written about 60 A.D. during Paul's imprisonment in Rome, the letter instructs us about forgiveness and accepting our fellow Christians as our equals, no matter what their perceived class might be. The homeless man in the mission shelter is as much our equal in Christ as the wealthiest member of the congregation. This is the teaching, but not often the practice.

Onesimus stole from Philemon when he ran away. He ran to Rome where he learned of Paul and had the opportunity to hear him preach. Onesimus was converted to Christianity and faced a serious challenge in his new life. He knew he had to set the account straight with Philemon, but risked the penalty of death for his crimes. Paul intervened on the behalf of Onesimus by sending this epistle with him to Philemon.

A mere 26 verses long, the letter packs a strong punch. The Book of Philemon is a work of applied Christianity. Paul wisely opens his letter to Philemon with a reminder that he is a prisoner. He has an understanding of Onesimus' position as a slave. Paul makes no social commentary on the ethic of owning slaves, but he does gently remind Philemon he is a captive, too. (Vs. 1 and Vs. 9) Paul does make it clear Christianity can never sanction slavery. Christ came to set the captives free and make Christians equal.

In verses 16 and 17, Paul urges Philemon to receive Onesimus as his brother rather than his servant. Even though Onesimus had stolen from Philemon, Paul tells him to receive him back as he would because people do change. Paul, formerly known as Saul, was the ex Murderer and chief persecutor of the church. Now as a chief Apostle and author of the majority of the New Testament, Paul was a first hand witness to that fact.

There is an age old saying that a leopard cannot change its spots (Jeremiah 13:23) as if to say "People don't Change". The saying "people don't change" is harmful and one of the most untruthful statement made because it denies the possibility of redemption.

There is something profound about the redeemed. The man who has experienced the lowest level of existence and conquered his personal demons has an empathy sadly lacking in more 'saintly' people. In a society supposedly built on the Christian doctrine of forgiveness, it is remarkable how eager we are to label people as permanent degenerates.

Circumstances and hardships sometimes lead good people to do foolish things. To say those mistakes are irredeemable is hypocritical. If the world considered only your most depraved moments, how would you be judged? People do change.

We make every decision for the first time with no obligation to the past. If we control anything, we control our own thoughts and behavior. If we can improve anything, it should be ourselves. So today, before you judge someone or decide to hold something against someone, take a look at the man in the mirror (yourself). Look how far you have come, how you have grown, the wrongs you have made right. Look at the smile that once was a frown, the joy in your heart that once was full of sorrow, the old bitter heart that is now open to give and receive love. Most of all, look at the old sinner now saved by God's precious grace.

Before you decide to throw someone away and cut them off forever, just remember people will never be perfect but <u>people do change</u>. The proof of that is - you did!

Fresh Wind

Hebrews 1 – James 2

My spirit compels me to repeat an illustration the Holy Spirit gave me during one of the services at Empowerment Temple. In the sermon entitled, *"I Tried To Keep It Together"* from Acts 27, I spoke about the frustration one experiences when you are on track to do the will of the Master, but things are not going at the pace you desire.

Paul is trying to make his way to see the ruler in order to lend his testimony; however, the boat he is on seems to be going just a mile a minute. It would seem plausible for things to go slow when you have no direction or clear cut destiny. It is all the more intolerable to know you have somewhere to go, but the pace you are keeping is not commensurate. The job offers are not coming, yet you know you are not lazy, but qualified and industrious. The dates are not coming when God has gifted you to be a great mate. The ministry opportunities just are not there and you have a gift in you that must be shared!

Paul tells us things were not going good until a storm came and the storm was precipitated by wind. Ironically, it was the wind and storm which helped the ship to pick up the pace and begin to move. Sometimes it is your storm that will give you the push you need to make it.

I shared with the congregants that in my travels to the West Coast both to preach and to visit my parents, I discovered its quicker going out to the west coast than it is to fly back to the East Coast. Then I remembered the pilot on one occasion announcing that we were making it in ahead of schedule because a tail wind was pushing us! What a revelation to know there was a wind pushing and assisting us, not just to make it, but to make it ahead of schedule.

Imagine my heart leap when I rose this morning to do today's reading and can not get any further than Hebrews 1:7 where it says, "He makes His angels winds!" Put your foot on the break. God makes His angels the wind! That changes everything!

I must go back and reevaluate all that I have read over the past 80 days. That insight helps me to better understand the story of Ezekiel when the Lord took him to the valley of dry bones and the Lord asked him if the bones could live. Ezekiel retorted back, "Lord, thou knowest." In return God told him to prophesy to the bones and the bones began to come together because of the wind angels. So angels are assisting in bringing together the fragmented areas of my life.

What about when the prophet was on the run and in a mountain nook looking and listening for God? An earthquake came, but God was not in the earthquake. Then the wind, but God was not in the wind (angels). This could cause a Biblical tug of war because do not forget, Satan is a fallen angel; so maybe the wind that came by on that dog day afternoon was the presence of something very ungodly. Do not get it twisted!

What about those who sat by the pool waiting on the troubling of the water, or the wind from an angel to cause a wave so one might get healed? Or even the instance where the disciples were caught in a tempestuous storm, but Jesus said to the wind and the waves, "*Peace! Be still!*" It makes sense now that the angels had to follow the orders of their boss. So when we get to Acts 27, Paul made progress on that ship because of the aid and assistance of the angels.

Whenever there is a hot and humid day, you hope for a fresh wind to lend some relief. I pray right now for you that on this day, under the relentless heat of your everyday travels, you will experience a fresh wind (visitation of angels). I am going right now to turn off my air conditioner and open the windows in hopes angels will come through my house and carry a breath of fresh air!

The Internet Altar

James 3 - 3 John

Over the last 85 days, we have grown together as a family in a very real way. We have fasted together, cried together, changed, developed and matured. As we come to the end of this journey, I feel compelled to open up the altar for prayer. There are countless numbers of you who are going through some serious tight spots and challenges and it is my earnest prayer you do no conclude these 90 days the same way you started.

13 Is any among you afflicted? Let him pray. Is any merry? Let him sing psalms.

14 Is any sick among you? Let him call for the elders of the church, and let them pray over him, anointing him with oil in the name of the Lord.

15 And the prayer of faith shall save the sick, and the Lord shall raise him up. And if he have committed sins, they shall be forgiven him.

16 Confess *your* faults one to another, and pray one for another, that ye may be healed. The effectual fervent prayer of a righteous man availeth much.

James 5:13-16

Today, my staff and I want to pray with you and over you. I believe in the power of the Word and I believe in the power of prayer. Make your prayer needs and concerns known today and we will be lifting up the situation on the altar. All day I charge you to pray one for another and believe God is going to do His perfect work. The text says, "Pray for those who are sick,"

(James 5:14), so for all intensive purposes, we are not limiting the prayer to just physical sickness, but whatever it is you might be sick of - the altar is now open! You may submit your request to: prayer@empowermenttemple.org

It's Not Over!

Jude – Revelation 17

Yesterday we hit a milestone mark in our journey to completing the Bible in 90 days. I have been interacting with you through these devotions for the whole process and never have we had a response like the one for the Internet Altar. This response said several things to me; 1) the body of Christ is truly going through travail in this hour in a real way and 2) healing is happening on many levels.

Last night when we gathered for Bible study, the spirit of intercession hovered over us like a cloud. It was almost as if the prayers going up were being met in mid air with the prayers that were coming down. You ought not to look at this as an ending but rather a beginning. I find it intriguing that when you have come to the end of a prescribed course work, it is not referred to as a conclusion, but rather a commencement, which is a beginning. As we come to the end of our reading, it is not our conclusion but rather our beginning. Our reading today makes it abundantly clear.

A book that is often ignored and overlooked and easily passed is the book of Jude. It is the next to the last book in the Bible and is a letter which consists of only 25 verses. It's a letter of admonishment, encouragement and direction. You can tell by the wording Jude has the heart of a pastor. He encourages us in verse three to fight and keep our faith.

In verses 5-7, he almost verbatim echoes the sentiment of 2 Peter by reminding us what happens to those who take God's grace for granted.

In verse 9, he gives and shows us that even in death; there is a fight for us. Your stock has to go up knowing the devil wants you dead or alive!

In verse 17, Jude tells us to remember the prophecies and promises over our lives.

In verse 20, he tells us to build ourselves up in prayer as we did yesterday, because there is yet a journey in front of us to be climbed.

In verse 21-23, he gives us marching orders, *"keep yourselves in God's love as you wait for the mercy of our Lord Jesus Christ to bring you to eternal life. Be merciful to those who doubt; snatch others from the fire and save them; to others show mercy, mixed with fear—hating even the clothing stained by corrupted flesh"*.

That seems to be the end of the sermon, but Jude has something even more profound to say when he declares a benediction in verses 24-25, *"To him who is able to keep you from falling and to present you before his glorious presence without fault and with great joy— to the only God our Savior be glory, majesty, power and authority, through Jesus Christ our Lord, before all ages, now and forevermore! Amen"*.

When I give the benediction on Sundays and Tuesday night, it marks the end of the service. Therefore, it would seem appropriate that this is the end. It's not! Turn the page and you see...the revelation. My point is this, as we come to the end of our 90 days, get ready for the revelation. God is going to show you a revelation about your gifts, your future, your finance your family and your call. There are those who are going to come behind you in this 90-day process that will need a little encouragement like we found from our friend Jude. I want them to know what revelations you have received on this journey. Only bear and keep in mind that greater is coming later!

The Field Is Open

Revelation 18 - Revelations 22

You made it! This has been a blessed ninety days. We have grown in leaps and bounds, overcome great obstacles, climbed many mountains, swam through many oceans and seas and walked through valleys. Some days it felt like we were being beaten and crucified, yet we have triumphed through it all. During this journey we have uncovered so many mysteries and truths, but more importantly, we have learned our God and now we can and will do great exploits.

In today's reading, Revelation 22:7 it says, "Look, I am coming soon! Blessed are those who obey the words of prophecy written in this book". So no matter what each day holds, after these ninety days know that your dedication and sacrifice has not been in vain. Not only have you triumphed on Earth, but you have triumphed in Heaven. Now it is not enough for us to just be hearers of this Word, but now our charge from this day forth is to be doers of this Word. We have no more excuses, but we now have the POWER, wisdom and knowledge we need to demonstrate and dominate in every area of life. This journey is not over, but instead is just the beginning!

I want to speak a blessing over your life as we come to a close of these 90 days. Now all glory to God, who is able to keep you from falling away and will bring you with great joy into His glorious presence without a single fault. All glory to Him who alone is God, our Savior through Jesus Christ our Lord. All glory, majesty, power, and authority are His before all time, and in the present, and beyond all time! Amen.

During these 90 days, if no one else has told you they love you and they believe you, know that I do, and I will be praying for you every step of the way.

The field is open. Run on and do great things!

History – 6 books

- Matthew: this book presents Jesus as the Messiah. It chronicles the birth of Christ, His baptism, temptation and ministry. Also found is passage on future events. Genealogy of Jesus is listed through Joseph. Fulfillment of Old Testament prophecy

- Mark: presents Jesus as the Servant. Mark was written for Gentile and Roman readers. It centers on Christ and the service of the believer to Him. One-third of this gospel deals with the last week of Jesus' life.

- Luke: Presents Jesus as the Son of Man, to seek and save the lost. Genealogy of Jesus through Mary. Largest of the gospels. The theme of this book is also Christ and gives us a view of the Christ's compassion.

- John: reveals Jesus as God in flesh, the Christ, so you might believe. John deals mostly with the nature of Christ. It is a book about Him and about having faith in Him. He is the Son of God, yet He is hungry, thirsty, weary, felt pain, suffered death, and rose alive. John shows seven miracles of Christ: water into wine; the healing of the nobleman's son; healing of the paralyzed person; feeding of the multitude; walking on water; opening the blind eyes and the raising of Lazarus from the dead.

The Holy Spirit is spoken of and the new birth.

- Acts: a record of the Apostles as they journeyed to various parts of the world to deliver the message of the gospel of Christ and its deliverance to the world; as well as Christianity in Jerusalem, Palestine and Syria.

- Romans: speaks of justification by faith and what happens if faith is not present. The righteousness of God is shown and many things are discussed relating to Christianity. The confession of Christ as the Son of God grants salvation.

175

PAULINE EPISTLES - 12 books

- I Corinthians: the first letter written by Paul to the Corinthians. It deals with spirituality and morality. It speaks of the judgment seat of Christ, the temple of the Holy Spirit, the Lord's Supper, love, gifts and resurrection.

- II Corinthians: Paul's second letter to the Corinthians. It reveals the the joy Paul had when the church accepted his ministry. It also offers some insight into Paul's life. This letter also talks about giving.

- Galatians: talks about justification by faith. There is only one way for man to come to God—accept the death, burial and resurrection of Christ.

- Ephesians: written while Paul was in prison. This letter speaks of God's purpose in establishing the Church of Christ. Christ is spoken of as the head of the church. The church is spoken of as the building and temple of God and also as the Bride of Christ.

- Philippians: Paul was in prison at the writing of this letter also. This book speaks of self-denial, giving up self for Christ; as well as the importance of prayer - praying always, and in all things giving thanks.

- Colossians: a third book written from prison. Paul talks about the importance and supreme nature of Christ. We can find all things in Christ and in Him, we are drawn into union.

- I Thessalonians: Paul expresses his thankfulness to the church and talks about the rapture of the church, the last days and the day of the Lord.

- II Thessalonians: Sent by Paul because it seems the church misunderstood Paul's first letter pertaining to the coming of the day of the Lord. Paul speaks out against the idle talkers and clears up the message pertaining to the day of the Lord in its relation to the present, the believers and unbelievers. It exhorts the people to pray and stand in faithfulness and obedience.

- I Timothy: The main idea of this book is for the believer to fight the good fight. We are told how to act in the house of God. Rules and structure are given for bishops, elders, and deacons of the church. The book speaks also of the last days, caring for others and the use of money.

- II Timothy: Here in this book we are told how to be a good and faithful soldier of Christ. The last days, inspiration of the Words of God and the crown of righteousness are discussed. This book calls us to be courageous, faithful, strong, and loyal servants to God.

- Titus: Here we have the qualifications for the elders, operation of the church and the duties of the minister. An exhortation to be wary of false teachings and the working of the Holy Spirit is included.

- Philemon: This letter is also one that was written while Paul was in prison. This is a very personal letter which offers praise to Philemon, a plea, and pledge and speaks of personal things concerning Philemon.

NON PAULINE EPISTLES – 8 books

- Hebrews: This book speaks of the greatness of Christ. A great salvation is given to us, as are the throne of grace and the intercession of Christ for the believer. The writing also describes faith and gives a roll call of the heroes of faith.

- James: Emphasizes the believer's conduct. We are told how faith can work in our everyday life. Faith and works are the two main points of the book, followed closely by the tongue and prayer for the sick.

- I Peter: Thought to be written in Babylon (Rome) and is the depiction of the "true grace of God," in the believer. This book tells us grace includes security, submission, obedience, suffering, service, growth and love.

- II Peter: Here we see the inspiration of the scriptures and the assuredness of Christ's second coming. Peter talks of faith and false teachings. It gives the characteristics of false teachers and look at the future.

- I John: Devoted to the welfare of the spiritual life of the believer. It is full of comparisons of dark to light, the love of the world and the love of God. It speaks of the children of God and the children of Satan, in addition to the spirit of the antichrist and the Spirit of God.

- II John: The main idea in this book is to walk in the commandments of Christ. We are told to love one another, be cautious about false teachings and to walk in truth and love.

- III John: This is a personal letter addressed to Gaius discussing godly living and the treatment of traveling ministers.

- Jude: Jude says that he is the author of this book, the brother of James, and half brother of Jesus. The purpose of his writing is to show a defense of the faith developed by the apostles against the false teachings springing up in the churches. Jude exposes the false teachers and exhorts the believers.

Prophecy – 1 book

- Revelation: Jesus Christ is the center of this book and it is His revelation to John, written by John. It contains four principal views or interpretations: 1) Preterist - a view of prophecy as already being fulfilled; 2) Historical - a portrayal of church history from the days of John to the end of time. 3) Idealist - a picture of events as they are unfolding and in conflict. 4) Futurist - a view of the majority of the book having not yet happened. The book is one that is to be understood by those desiring to read it and gain its wisdom.

You have now been empowered. I now charge you to go and empower someone else. To change the world, you must first start by Empowering and Impacting a LIFE.

Personal Reflection

Personal Reflection

_____
_____
_____
_____
_____
_____
_____
_____
_____
_____
_____
_____
_____
_____
_____
_____
_____
_____
_____
_____
_____
_____

Dr. Jamal H. Bryant

About The Author

Radical, Revolutionary, Innovative, Anointed, and Cutting Edge are some of the words often used to describe Dr. Jamal-Harrison Bryant. This ministry driven vanguard has inspired thousands of believers around the nation. He has an unprecedented prophetic mantle that distinguishes him as a remarkable visionary who has made a powerful impact in the Christian Arena. Stepping out on faith, with 43 people who believed that God was going to do the unexpected, Dr. Bryant founded The Empowerment Temple. The first service was held on Easter Sunday, April 22, 2000, in a Baltimore City banquet hall. In just seven short years, God directed the paths of over 10,000 members to Empowerment Temple, the fastest growing church in the A.M.E. denomination.

Dr. Bryant is a pastor with a global mission, which is to "Empower the World through the Word." He believes that the body of Christ should be empowered in every area of life. His preaching and teaching focuses on empowering believers spiritually, developing them educationally, exposing them culturally, activating them politically, and strengthening them economically.

Prior to his role as pastor, Dr. Bryant served as the director of the NAACP's youth and college division. A dynamic motivational speaker, he was responsible for over 650 youth councils and college chapters, representing over 68,000 young people in the United States, Germany, and Japan. Today, his ecumenical messages have been heard on the far shores of South Africa, Belgium, England, and India. His contributions have been highlighted in numerous publications, including Ebony Magazine, Hope Today Magazine, Gospel Today Magazine, Emerge, Sister To Sister, USA Today, and The Source. In addition to his many prestigious highlights, Dr. Bryant has appeared on BET's Meet the Faith, CNN, C-Span, and Politically Incorrect. He also served as a panelist on the National town hall meeting entitled, "The State of Black America", and "The State of the Black Church", hosted by renowned author and talk show personality Tavis Smiley. According to Ebony Magazine, he is one of America's future leaders.

While Dr. Bryant has distinguished himself and attained great accomplishments, it is noteworthy to mention that he failed the 11th grade and dropped out of high school. However, he later obtained a GED certificate and went on to further his education. He received a bachelor's degree in Political Science and International Studies, from Morehouse College in Atlanta, Georgia, and earned a Master of Divinity degree from Duke University in Durham, North Carolina. In 2005 he received his Doctor of Ministry Degree.

With a mission to "Empower the World through the Word", the "Power for Life" broadcast is heard weekly across the United States, the Caribbean, England and throughout the continent of Africa. In 2003, The Empowerment Academy, an elementary school for grades Pre-K through 2nd, and The Empowerment Temple Family Life Center opened its doors to serve the community. The church has also registered more voters than any other church in Baltimore City. After three years of worshiping in several locations, a banquet hall, a college campus and a high school auditorium, on February 15, 2004, the

Empowerment Temple congregation triumphantly marched into its new 2,000 seat sanctuary located in Baltimore City. In spite of the awesome anointing on his life, Dr. Bryant is still modest enough to "keep it real." His humility allows him to connect with those from age seven to seventy.

He and his family happily live in Baltimore. No matter how he is described, Dr. Jamal-Harrison Bryant is "Empowering the World through the Word."